QUICKSILVER MESSENGER SERVICE & THE END OF AN ERA

QUICKSILVER MESSENGER SERVICE & THE END OF AN ERA

David R. Greenland

BearManor Media
2025

Quicksilver Messenger Service & the End of an Era

Published in the United States of America by:

BearManor Media

1317 Edgewater Dr. #110
Orlando, FL 32804

bearmanormedia.com

Printed in the United States.

Typesetting and layout by PKJ Passion Global

ISBN–979-8-88771-763-0

For Harriet, Patron Saint

PREFACE & ACKNOWLEDGMENTS

Whenever I come across a book regarding an aspect of popular culture—music, film, or television—I am always curious about the author's qualifications. Is the writer an expert on the subject, or merely a zealous admirer who has composed a highly biased valentine to the object of their passion?

With that in mind, what makes me eligible to write a chronicle of Quicksilver Messenger Service, a legendary San Francisco band whose history no one has yet recorded in a single volume? Let me offer this very abridged version of my relevant credentials:

I was born in the early 1950s and come from a family of music lovers and amateur musicians. My parents, brothers, and most of my relatives had larger than average record collections, so I grew up exposed to everything from Nat King Cole, Frank Sinatra, Tony Bennett, and Mahalia Jackson to, of course, Elvis Presley. What intrigued me the most, however, were my father's jazz albums: Louis Armstrong, Duke Ellington, Miles Davis, and several lesser known artists. From a very early age my brain was wired to appreciate music that was more adventurous than most of what was in the Top 40, especially pre-1964.How Miles Davis interpreted the old standard "Bye Bye Blackbird" in comparison to the rendition on one of those Mitch Miller sing-along albums struck me as nothing less than revelatory. Consequently, I was primed to accept the sounds that started coming from San Francisco in the late 1960s.

Like the Rolling Stones' Keith Richards, my first musical hero was Roy Rogers, but that changed once I acquired a transistor radio and discovered Ray Charles. (Nearly thirty years later, I attended the public ceremony when Brother Ray was given a star on the Hollywood Walk of Fame.) Of course I was a Beatlemaniac (the first album I bought with my own money was a mono copy of *Something*

New), an obsession which resulted in becoming part of several bands of varying sizes and styles for the next three decades. We played at parties and in coffee houses, and recorded in living rooms, basements, garages, and professional studios. By far my most significant musical achievement was having a track made with the late Barry Craig (known in ambient music circles as A Produce) ending up on a 2021 compilation CD released by Independent Projects Records. In his liner notes, veteran rock journalist David Fricke compared our contribution to David Crosby's first solo album, which happened to be one of our major inspirations.

Over the years I learned to play a few instruments—none exceptionally—and how to read and write music, but that was most definitely not the type of writing at which I excelled. Combining that talent with an addiction to music (leading to a collection of several thousand albums), my first efforts to see print—besides high school and college newspapers—were in the numerous rock publications that flourished in the late 1960s and into the '70s. Most of my submissions were rejected (someone at the once-essential Rolling Stone scrawled only "sorry" on one), a few were published, and I was once paid for a piece that was never used. I briefly found work as a reporter, taught a creative writing class at a local college, and wrote books devoted to vintage television series. Serendipitously, I discovered that one of my neighbors, Doug Cameron, had been a roadie for the Doors, and I persuaded him to let me help write his self-published memoir (*Inside the Fire: My Strange Days with the Doors*) of those days.

I've never been a rabid attendee of live concerts, but have managed to see many of the greats and other worthwhile artists from A (America) to Z (ZZ Top), a few more than once: Bob Dylan, the Grateful Dead, the Doors, CSN, Muddy Waters, B.B. King, Stevie Ray Vaughan, Dr. John, Mahavishnu Orchestra, Gordon Lightfoot, Kris Kristofferson, Roberta Flack, Merle Haggard, the Hollies, Willie Nelson, Johnny Cash, Chicago, Jackson Browne, Ry Cooder, the

Charlie Daniels Band, Wet Willie, Pure Prairie League, Waylon Jennings, Eric Clapton, Hamilton Camp and many more. In particular, Quicksilver Messenger Service put on two of the most rousing shows I've ever experienced.

The band was notoriously publicity-shy, granting few interviews during the peak of their popularity. "We weren't ambitious to make it big in the music business or anything," said guitarist/singer Gary Duncan in 2016. "We just wanted to play. We wanted to make enough money to pay the rent and have some pot to smoke." Nor were they interested in making records, becoming the last major San Francisco band to sign with a label. Even then they were not the subject of as much press coverage as Jefferson Airplane or the Grateful Dead. As a result, I've had to rely on my personal library of music-oriented books (which number in the hundreds) and a scant amount of articles and reviews in back issues of music publications, several of which went out of business decades ago. Needless to say, this book would not have been possible if not for the recollections and/or pioneering histories of Lee Abraham, Toni Brown, David Crosby, Shelley L. Duncan, David Gans, John Glatt, Ralph J. Gleason, Carl Gottlieb, Robert Greenfield, Christopher Hjort, Richard Morton Jack, Bill Kreutzmann, Phil Lesh, Andy McArthur,Dennis McNally, Ed Munsen, Mark Myers, Bruce Pollack, Peter Richardson, Sandy Troy, Jann S. Wenner, and Paul Williams.

This is certainly *not* a complete history of San Francisco's golden era as a musical mecca, a time more thoroughly and colorfully depicted by such indispensible works as Joel Selvin's *Summer of Love*, Charles Perry's *The Haight-Ashbury*, Jeff Tamarkin's *Got A Revolution!: The Turbulent Flight of Jefferson Airplane*, Blair Jackson's *Garcia: An American Life*, *Living With The Dead* by Rock Scully and David Dalton, Craig Fenton's *Take Me to A Circus Tent: The Jefferson Airplane Flight Log* and Julian Dawson's *...and on piano Nicky Hopkins* in particular.

A considerable amount of information about Quicksilver Messenger Service in magazines, books, liner notes, and the Internet is redundant and/or inaccurate, so I am exceptionally indebted to devoted Quicksilver fans/journalists David Cavanagh, Ed Condran, Bill DeYoung, Mike Fornatale, John Kirkman, Arthur Levy, Dan MacIntosh, Jon "Mojo" Mills, Joli Valenti Powers, Alan Robinson, Michael Saltzman, Dean Sciarra, Mick Skidmore, Mark Skobac, Mike Somavilla, George Starostin, Dave Thompson, John Tobler, and Richie Unterberger. Particular appreciation is extended to Jeff Tamarkin for his concise essay in Culture Shock's rare 2015 Quicksilver box set.

Special thanks to Natalie Snoyman of the Lucretia Little History Room of the Mill Valley Public Library for permission to quote from Debra Schwartz's 2019 interview with David Freiberg, and for efforts to put me in touch with Mr. Freiberg.

Enormous gratitude to the following companies: Air Cuts/ODL, Bear Records/Voiceprint, BGO Records, Capitol Records, Carlotta's CDs, Cema Special Markets, Charly Records, Cleopatra Records/Purple Pyramid Records, Collectors' Choice Music, Floating World/Retro World, Freakbeat Records, Gary Duncan Archives, Global World Ltd., Gonzo Multimedia, It'sABoutMusic, LLC, Koch International/Sony Music, Lab Records/Great American Music Company, Mig Music, Pymander Records, Sonic Boom, and Soundstage/ODL. Very special thanks to Keith Martin!

All photographs are from the author's personal collection, some courtesy of various record labels, and others in the public domain. The author claims no ownership of any images.

Thanks also to the assistance or encouragement of Paul Greenland, Steve "Bro" Homan, Ben Ohmart, Sarah Joseph, Nick Anez, and, as ever, my wife Cleo, whose open mind, open ears, and extreme patience contributed greatly to the realization of this project.

*

INTRODUCTION

"We would all like to be able to live an uncluttered life, a simple life, a good life, you know, and, like, think about moving the whole human race a step ahead. Or a few steps. Or half a step."

Jerry Garcia of The Grateful Dead, 1967

A musical renaissance that endured at least through 1974 began in 1965, the year simple rock 'n' roll began its transformation into rock. No longer was youth-oriented music merely for the feet ("It has a good beat, and you can dance to it," said countless teen judges on Dick Clark's *American Bandstand*), but also for the head. Lyrics meant something and were often poetic, even controversial. Most responsible for this change was a combination of the early '60s folk boom, led by Bob Dylan, and the so-called British Invasion of 1964, with the Beatles at the forefront. A comparison of the charts from 1963 and those of 1965 illustrates how quickly and dramatically the musical landscape shifted. Gone were the likes of Chubby Checker, Little Peggy March, and Hollywood teen idols like Paul Peterson. The best-selling fifty albums of 1965 still included movie and Broadway soundtracks (which would continue to dominate until 1968), but also such landmark recordings as *Bringing It All Back Home* and *Highway 61 Revisited* (both featuring Dylan's first use of electric instruments), *The Beach Boys Today!* (Brian Wilson's first serious attempts to move beyond songs about surfing and cars), three by the Rolling Stones (*The Rolling Stones, Now!, 12x5, Out of Our Heads*), and three by the Beatles (*Beatles '65, Beatles VI, A Hard Day's Night*), who had managed to notch the biggest seller of the previous year (*Meet the Beatles*), a first for a pop group. Joan Baez, the Supremes, and Peter, Paul & Mary also made respectable showings.

While it remains true that there are really only two kinds of music—good and bad—a cornucopia of sounds was emanating from the United Kingdom and all across the United States: New York, Chicago, Detroit, Memphis, Nashville, Los Angeles, and San Francisco. For ten years, blues, folk, country, soul, jazz, and pop all coalesced in the entity known as rock. Incredibly, all of these styles coexisted more or less comfortably, appealing—to varying degrees—to everyone listening. Thus could singer/songwriter Laura Nyro and Quicksilver Messenger Service perform on the same day at the Monterey Pop Festival in 1967 and be appreciated by the same audience. Ditto for the Woodstock Music & Art Fair two years later, where Joan Baez and Ravi Shankar were both accepted by the masses. (Imagine Taylor Swift and the Foo Fighters on the same bill today and being cheered equally by their wildly diverse fans. More than likely it will never happen.)

Baby Boomers—anyone born between 1946 and 1964—in their teens and twenties by 1965 came of age along with the roughly ten-year development of what is now known as Classic Rock. (Some disc jockeys insist on extending this time frame into the 1980s, arguably the most dated and artificial decade in music history, a great many of its albums—including good ones—overproduced, sterile, and outright dull.) Several musicologists have suggested that the music one hears between the ages of thirteen and thirty tends to make the most vivid impression, so it is not surprising that most Boomers I know regard the Classic Rock period as paramount. Never before and never again was such an amazing variety of music created.

But what accounts for generations not even born during those years regarding the late '60s/early '70s as a magic time, when groundbreaking albums were being released on an almost weekly basis? Philosopher Tobias Churton, author of *The Spiritual Meaning of the Sixties*, observes:

"My daughter was born in 2000. At a certain point in her teens she began collecting vinyl records: largely re-releases of 'seminal'

1960s music by the Beatles, the Who, the Band, the Byrds, the Rolling Stones, Pink Floyd, Jimi Hendrix, and the Doors...She 'dug' it because it spoke directly to her in a way much contemporary popular music did not—and the contemporary music she *did*—and does—buy into undoubtedly drew inspiration from the best of Sixties pop/rock. Among my daughter's friends who share her enthusiasm subsists a common belief that 'the Sixties' was something they are very annoyed to have missed, even something they might have preferred to have been born into. Still, something of 'it' may yet be accessed through music, not out of nostalgia or, obviously, wistful reminiscence, but of immediate delight. The music seems to these young people very 'now,' fresh, of the moment, even vital and superior."

In the late '90s I was managing a used CD store, and while discs by the latest one-hit wonders and flavors-of-the-month sat accumulating dust, albums released during the late '60s/early '70s were rarely brought in. When they were, their shelf life was always limited. I recall a young man no older than sixteen or seventeen who was buying titles by the Doors, Savoy Brown, the Grateful Dead, and a few others, saying, "Man, I'm sure glad I found these. Today's music sucks!" When I told him I had passed up an opportunity to go to Woodstock, his eyes widened and he shook his head. "Man, you were dumb! Were you ever in San Francisco?" "In spirit," I replied. He seemed to be impressed that I heard the first Santana album before it was released because a woman I worked with knew someone in the band and had an advance copy.

I am now what some acquaintances call an aging hippie, but I certainly did not *look* like one in high school. (With black frame glasses and short hair I could have passed for Buddy Holly's cousin.) Even so, I tended to hang around with students who did, who were attracted to and affected by the new music, who had a genuine concern for what was making the world an ugly place: war, racism, assassinations, politics, destruction of the ecology, corporate greed, rampant materialism, the hypocrisy of organized religion, subjugation of women, —all societal problems that, unfortunately, have yet to be fully eradicated. The belief among some young people that anyone over thirty could not be trusted was naïve, but not as asinine as the slogans adopted by right-wing conservatives (a/k/a The Establishment): America, love it or leave it; my country, right or wrong; make America beautiful—get a haircut. The aptly named Generation Gap seemed to widen in direct proportion to the escalation of the government's disastrous misadventure in Vietnam. The specter of that war hung over the heads of all young men who had to register for the draft and face the possibility of their future being put on hold. Music became a welcome and even necessary distraction, if not a refuge.

Fortunately, the high school I attended was fairly liberal in that the student council was allowed to pipe music into the cafeteria during lunch hour, which is where I'm reasonably certain I first heard Quicksilver Messenger Service one afternoon in early 1969. "This here is rock and roll," a voice muttered, followed by a bone-crunching rendition of Bo Diddley's "Mona," punctuated by a stinging, almost trembling lead guitar, the likes of which I had never heard before. No one I was sitting with knew who it was, but we all agreed it was amazingly different than what was played before or after. At the end of the day, the girl whose locker was next to mine appeared with an armload of albums, and the cover of the one on top was an antiquated painting of a mounted cowboy waving farewell to a pioneer woman in the distance. It was called *Happy Trails*, a famous number by my early hero Roy Rogers, and the band was Quicksilver Messenger Service. "Do they do that old song?" I asked. "At the end," she replied. "Kind of corny, but the rest is great!" She confirmed that "Mona" was one of the tracks. I had my own copy before the week was out.

***"In 1967, young people were united in their opposition to the war and discovering the music that unified them. Jimi Hendrix and Janis Joplin were not pop idols. They were part of a movement, and we were all in it together."* Neil Young, 2007**

In those days, San Francisco had a thriving music scene made up of artists for whom fame and fortune were not their highest priorities, unlike most of the aspiring musicians in Los Angeles. (Notable exceptions were the Byrds, Buffalo Springfield, Love, Canned Heat, and the Doors.) Many Bay Area musicians regarded the music business with suspicion, and having a hit record was viewed as a form of "selling out" to commercialism. Early in their career, the members of Quicksilver Messenger Service were not even much interested in performing anywhere outside California. There was a spirit of camaraderie and exploration among the nearly 300 bands that existed by the middle of 1969, chief among them Jefferson Airplane, the Grateful Dead, Big Brother & the Holding Company, Country Joe & the Fish, and Quicksilver Messenger Service, the latter most influenced by blues and jazz. "We weren't your typical folk-rock band," said guitarist/singer Gary Duncan. "We played blues, r'n'b, rock'n'roll...and yes, a few folk songs...We played really loud and we had a *groove*. If you wanted to dance, you could dance to us. The major difference between us, the Airplane and the Dead was that we had the best rhythm section in the city." Unlike pop/rock bands, they each had a distinctive sound. The Airplane's Grace Slick sounded nothing like Big Brother's Janis Joplin. Lead guitarists Jorma Kaukonen (Airplane), Jerry Garcia (Dead), John Cipollina and Duncan (Quicksilver) were uniquely different in their approach and tone. Their concerts emphasized substance over style, relied on nothing more than a simple light show rather than props, lasers, and dancers to enhance what the music lacked—because the music lacked nothing. By contrast, many of today's most popular "artists" are, in fact, not artists at all, merely marginally talented entertainers dependent on flashy costumes and elaborate special effects to compensate for unimaginative material. The real "stars" of their recordings are the producers and engineers who use a variety of digital tricks to make up for vapid music and insipid lyrics. (In 2003, Roger Davies, manager of Tina Turner and Joe Cocker, complained, "There seems to be a drought of great songs nowadays." It goes on.) This, happily, is not true of all musicians working today, none of them eager to land on *The Voice*, *American Idol* or *America's Got Talent*. Exceptional music is being made in the fields of blues and jazz, as well as what has come to be known as Americana, or roots music. Musicologist Nolan Gasser, in his massive study *Why You Like It: The Science & Culture of Musical Taste*, writes:

"A good part of what motivates the authenticity of rock music is its perennial drive back to 'the roots'—the almost mythological purity of those raw and rebellious early days of rock and roll: reckless teens playing simple, hard-driving songs in an old, beat-up garage."

The better contemporary artists are just that: authentic, blending all sorts of "earthy" sounds into a mix that emerges as timeless. And the same can be said of the San Francisco bands who left a lasting imprint on the last half of the Sixties, their occasional forays into psychedelic territory (some might say excess) now sounding less dated than the cold, soulless music of the 1980s. Even some Sixties albums that were disappointing at the time (*Dr. Byrds & Mr. Hyde* by the Byrds, *The Soft Parade* by the Doors, *At Your Birthday Party* by Steppenwolf) seem better in comparison to a lot of what was to come.

Not too many years ago, jazz trumpeter/composer Wynton Marsalis bravely but correctly said it was possible that all of the greatest jazz had already been created, that all that follows will be variations of what came before. It is a debatable opinion that can apply to any type of music, but as long as musicians continue to turn to such icons as Robert Johnson, Louis Armstrong, Bessie Smith, Hank Williams, Miles Davis, Ray Charles, Chuck Berry, Elvis Presley,

Bob Dylan, Muddy Waters, the Rolling Stones, and the Beatles—to name a dozen, but definitely not all, of the obvious examples—and not the likes of Britney Spears (whose music the late David Crosby accurately called "as deep as a birdbath")—rewarding rock music will not fade away. To be accurate, the solo artists and bands that emerged throughout the late '60s/early '70s were inspired by the legendary originators of blues, jazz, folk, country, and rock 'n' roll dating all the way back to the 1920s and before. An abundance of what was done during the 1980s and after was based on what was created in the previous two decades; no doubt there are, for example, members of Generation X who, unless they have a knowledgeable older sibling or friend, believe that the blues was invented by Led Zeppelin and would not have a clue who Howlin' Wolf or Willie Dixon were. Chalk that up to the birth of MTV and the homogenous nature of corporately-owned FM radio, which continues to this day. Long gone are the days when a pioneering San Francisco disc jockey by the name of Tom Donahue was free to play John Coltrane back-to-back with a ten-minute track by the Grateful Dead without some station owner in a three-piece suit ordering him to stick to a pre-approved/narrow-minded play list.

To date, Quicksilver Messenger Service, despite being one of the very few genuinely iconic San Francisco bands, has never been the subject of a complete account, or as nearly complete as is now possible, given that most of the original members are no longer with us. Until now, their story has been told in largely general terms, often mentioned only in passing in autobiographies, biographies, music-related books, and liner notes, a mere footnote in rock history. They were never nominated for a Grammy, never had a blockbuster single, and most likely will never be inducted into the Rock and Roll Hall of Fame. (As for why the band never achieved the same acclaim as Jefferson Airplane or the Grateful Dead, bass/viola player David Freiberg told *Relix* magazine in 2023, "I don't think we toured enough.") But from 1968 to 1975 they recorded eight diverse, substantial, and generally underrated albums for Capitol Records that have stood the proverbial test of time, especially among their loyal following. Even their lesser efforts are generally more interesting in comparison to current sounds. And in addition to anthologies of varying sizes, there are no less than 20 live recordings available from independent labels, though some of the venues and dates are wrong and the sound quality is generally less than state-of-the-art. The power of the music, however, always burns through the audio murk, the inferior discs sounding best when heard on headphones.

Again, this book is certainly not an attempt to tell the full story of San Francisco—or even Quicksilver Messenger Service—in the years when music mattered because it was saying something worth hearing, exploring different sounds, experimenting with uncommon instruments. Nor am I concerned with the private lives of the members of Quicksilver apart from how personal issues affected their music. And a passion for their music is the primary reason for this book. What they contributed to popular culture is long overdue for reassessment and appreciation. The history of the band, however blurred and contradictory it is at times, is a saga well worth telling.

*

1960-66

DINO

"...Dino Valenti, who is a great person to be on a bill with, since he will go up every set and just sing his ass off, y'know. Unless he is on some kind of change, he will usually go up and just really do his level best to stir your brains around with a spoon. He's a very live cat, y'know."

David Crosby, 1970

Chester William Powers, Jr. was born in Danbury, Connecticut, on October 7 in either 1937 or 1943. So were Chet Powers, Jesse Otis Farrow, Jesse Oris Farrow, and Dino Valente, all aliases of the singer/songwriter who ultimately found fame as Dino Valenti (the spelling that will be used in this book), composer of the beloved Sixties anthem "Get Together," sometimes known as "Let's Get Together." There has always been an air of mystery surrounding Dino. One rock scribe even claimed his middle name was not William, but simply A. In 1968 Dino told journalist Ralph J. Gleason, "I was raised on carnivals all along the East Coast and ran away to New York when I was 17. My parents were carnival people." Some in the musical community doubted the veracity of the statement, suspecting this claim was an attempt to make his background sound more fascinating than the truth. More than forty years later, his son, Joli Valenti Powers, settled the dispute. "My father was raised almost from birth on the carnival circuit by his vaudeville parents," he wrote in the liner notes for a CD of Dino's previously unreleased recordings. "His father, a champion ukulele player, had him loving the strings early on. My dad once told me his first instrument was a half-sized, pink Roy Rogers guitar. He began listening to gypsy music and the occasional black blues players that would come and go through the carnival along the way." More than twenty years after Dino's death in 1994, Gary Duncan told Uncut magazine, "Dino was born and raised on a carnival. He was a carny. He hustled everything and everybody—it was in his nature, he couldn't help it. He and I were partners for ten years, and in that time he got the reputation of being an egotist, which he was, and a narcissist, which he was, and a brutal person who did bad things to people. But when you got to know him, you realized that he was actually just a guy of simple intelligence who did a lot of stupid things. Dino had plenty of opportunities to do well in the business...He was so obnoxious to deal with that nobody wanted anything to do with him." Considering Dino's unsettled upbringing and several lengthy stretches behind bars, it is not surprising he developed an abrasive, Jekyll and Hyde personality. But it is also true that he was more musically gifted than has usually been acknowledged.

Following the death of his father, Dino enlisted in the United States Air Force, but military service was not a good fit for the aspiring troubadour, who was too much an individualist and soon drummed out. During the late 1950s he played with rock and roll combos in any bar that would hire them, but that path led nowhere. It was in the early 1960s, when the folk movement was in full flower, that Dino started his musical journey, armed with a twelve-string guitar. Such artists as Joan Baez, the Kingston Trio, the Limelighters, the Chad Mitchell Trio, the New Christy Minstrels, and Peter, Paul & Mary were making their mark with the general public, not just East Coast bohemians crowding the smoky coffeehouses of Greenwich Village, Boston, Provincetown, North Beach, and others. The East Village was Dino's destination, circa 1960, and immediately upon his arrival he began singing in the park.

Nearly a decade later he claimed that his first club gig lasted twelve hours. In short order he gained the reputation as the "underground Dylan" and was performing on the same stages as luminaries Tom Paxton, Fred Neil, Josh White, Hamilton Camp, and Richie Havens, who was known to play a few of Dino's compositions. Coffeehouses like the Dragon's Den and the renowned Café Wha? grew in popularity, so New York began requiring entertainers to apply for a cabaret license. Unfortunately, an arrest for some now-forgotten infraction disqualified Dino from obtaining one. After recording a single he called "Birdses" (its flip side "Don't Let It Down") for Elektra Records, he decided to head out to Los Angeles. (Future Byrd Gene Clark, then with the New Christy Minstrels, heard "Birdses" and, in late 1964, his memory of it allegedly inspired the name of the iconic band.)

It was 1963 when Dino arrived on the West Coast, a year radio was dominated by the surf music of The Beach Boys and Jan & Dean and easy listening tunes crooned by the likes of Bobby Vinton, Andy Williams, Steve Lawrence, and Al Martino. The only hits remotely similar to what Dino was doing were "If I Had a Hammer" by Trini Lopez and Peter, Paul & Mary's version of Dylan's "Blowin' In The Wind." He passed the time by performing solo and, briefly, with a band that included future Byrds drummer Michael Clarke. While living in New York, he had been offered a recording contract by more than one label, but according to Joli, "...his Carney ways left him to trust no one." In Los Angeles, however, a record producer by the name of Jim Dickson heard Dino in a club and asked if he would be interested in taping some of his songs for World Pacific, a jazz label that was branching out to include folk music. With success proving to be elusive, Dino took advantage of the opportunity. Dickson, who along with accountant Ed Tickner owned Tickson Music, provided Dino with a modicum of financial security by publishing the immortal "Get Together" (written that summer), first advancing him $100 for an overdue car payment. The song was destined to be covered by numerous other artists (We Five, Jefferson Airplane, the Youngbloods among them), first by the Kingston Trio on their Capitol album *Back in Town* (May 1964).

One might reasonably assume the royalties would ensure that Dino was set for life. But one would be wrong. Fated to frequently run afoul of the law, he was forced to sell the rights back to Dickson and Tickner to pay legal fees.

Dickson recorded another early version of "Get Together" by a pre-Byrds David Crosby, unreleased for thirty-seven years. Before that session took place, Crosby met Dino, a pre-Jefferson Airplane Paul Kantner, and a pre-Quicksilver David Freiberg in Sausalito, located north in Marin County. Now wearing a black cape, his confident swagger matching the forceful way he played guitar, Dino had acquired several girlfriends who were to inspire many of his compositions. Luckily, recent surgery to excise some knotted veins from his brain had done nothing to affect his creativity, though a similar affliction would recur many years later. He and Crosby, living in a no longer seaworthy ferryboat doubling as a folk den, explored unusual guitar chords and wrote a batch of songs, often working long into the night. A local musician who sometimes stopped by was John Cipollina, destined to become one of Quicksilver's lead guitarists. Crosby and Freiberg hitchhiked down to Los Angeles to escape the winter weather of northern California, eventually settling in Venice Beach, joined by Kantner. Crosby eventually became an integral part of a group known variously as the Beefeaters and the Jet Set before becoming The Byrds, a name chosen in November 1964. A 1969 article in Rolling Stone said Crosby allegedly asked

Dino to join him in the Byrds; the band did record Dino's "I Don't Want To Spoil Your Party"—more famously known as Quicksilver's "Dino's Song"—but it has never been released.

One song the band covered (and would record for their third album, *Fifth Dimension*, in 1966) was "Hey Joe," which Dino had taught Crosby, who thought it was a Valenti original but was actually written in 1962 by a Washington, D.C. folksinger, Billy James. According to legend, authorship was also claimed by folkie Tim Rose and one of James' former girlfriends, when in truth it was, like many traditional folk and blues songs, a variation of a timeworn ballad handed down through several generations. An apocryphal tale has Dino, then a "guest" of the state of California, convincing James to sign the rights to the song over to him as a way to demonstrate to the Folsom Prison parole board that he was a professional musician. Roberts later negotiated a deal to have the copyright reassigned to him, and of the many versions recorded since 1966 (first by The Leaves), including those by the Byrds and Jimi Hendrix, cite B. James, not Dino Valenti, as the composer.

Dino was back in Los Angeles by early 1965 and with Crosby rented a house in Laurel Canyon. The Byrds, after first recording several tracks for Jim Dickson at World Pacific Studios that would not be released until 1969, were signed by Columbia Records. Sessions for their debut album had begun, but all the members were keeping their options open. Crosby continued as a solo act at a club called the New Balladeer. Group leader Roger—then going by Jim—was increasingly attracted to technology. Aware of this, Dino approached him with a bizarre notion. "He had this great idea for a group," McGuinn recalled later. "He had designed costumes with radio transmitters built into the jackets, a place in your belt buckle to plug into your guitar, and it was a workable idea…But in the end I decided not to go along with him." It was not the last time Dino would suggest the concept.

Forever restless, conceivably a result of his rootless youth, Dino returned to the San Francisco Bay Area during the early summer of 1965. The stash of unreleased Valenti recordings begun at World Pacific Studios continued to grow when he cut some tracks for Autumn Records, a small label co-owned by former disc jockeys Bob Mitchell and Tom Donahue. (After taping the earliest studio efforts by the Grateful Dead, Donahue moved from Top 40 station KSAN to KMPX, where he became the "godfather" of free form FM radio, known as "underground" radio due to its programming music no Top 40 station would touch. Donahue, who became Dino's manager, once remarked, "Dino's one of the few American singers around who have a real capacity to sing to chicks.") Dino's cache of World Pacific and Autumn sessions, as well as some Quicksilver demos, remaining unheard for so many years was, said his son, due to "…my dad's own distrust of anyone that caused him to lock up his treasures in storage units all over northern California. Every time he moved, he put more stuff in storage. At times he would call me up and say, 'Hey, Joli! I got these keys to storage units but I can't remember where the units are.' So I would hit the yellow pages and always find them. Unfortunately sometimes they were already sold. So down the river went his favorite boots, jackets, pictures, 'girlfriends of the past' stuff and unfortunately one of them contained all his tapes." Not all, as it turned out, but it took literally decades to discover them.

*

DAVID

"David was a joyful sprite; a warm spirited, loving soul with the gift to enjoy life to its fullest. No matter what was going on, you could depend on David to approach every issue with common sense and a healthy dose of humor."

Shelley L. Duncan, 2002

David Freiberg, long regarded as one of the most amiable artists to emerge from the halcyon era of San Francisco music, fell in love with the city around the age of fifteen, long before becoming one of its residents. "On a family trip, we went through the West with four kids and two adults in the car," he recalled in 2019. "It was really good. We went to all the national parks and everything, then drove into San Francisco. And as we came around the 101, all of a sudden the fog was just starting to come in 'cause it was summer, and it was just so gorgeous. I said, 'I've gotta live in this place.' And I never forgot that."

Born in Boston, Massachusetts, in 1938, he developed an interest in music very early, taking violin lessons at the age of four after attending a children's concert by the Boston Pops. He spent most of his youth in Cincinnati, Ohio, where his family moved after David's father, an orthopedic surgeon, joined the navy when the Second World War broke out. Considering himself merely an average violinist, he switched to the viola, which he preferred. "I loved it," he said. "I loved the tone, and went crazy, and all of a sudden I was the first violist" in his junior high orchestra. He later became a member of Ohio's state orchestra and was part of a string quartet. Although he also played the cello and, eventually, the guitar and bass, his affinity for the viola never waned, its sound later enhancing more than a few tracks by Quicksilver. He can be seen with the instrument on the back cover of *Happy Trails* and inside the *Shady Grove* album, both 1969. In 1959, then twenty-one, he was working as a lost package tracker for a trucking company, attending college, and newly married. Intending to accept a position with a West Coast associate of his employer, his true aim was to finally realize his dream of moving to San Francisco. He and his wife "took the San Francisco Chief out of Chicago on Christmas Eve…and ended up living in Oakland. And the trucking job didn't work out, and the first job I could find to work on was at a pawn shop in downtown Oakland." His affinity for the railroad led to a job with Southern Pacific and a move to San Francisco.

By 1962, David's wife left him, "just disappeared one day." He filled that void in his life by buying a guitar and concentrating on his love of folk music, Pete Seger and the Weavers in particular. After taking his turn at the microphone in coffee houses on hootenanny nights, he linked up with an outfit called Folk Singers for

Peace. The proposed group turned out to be only a trio consisting of David, a young woman named Sandy, and Michael, a former Marine. "We were going to travel without money down through Mexico, all the way down through South America, living with the people, for peace and brotherhood, to spread peace and brotherhood. And that sounded like a nice thing to do." David convinced Southern Pacific to grant him a leave of absence. In Mexico City, where he first tried marijuana, they set up in parks, performing such popular folk numbers as "If I Had a Hammer" before being jailed one night as left-wing agitators. The following morning, the Mexican officials put them on an American Airlines flight headed for San Antonio, Texas, where they met Chet Helms, owner of San

Francisco's Avalon Ballroom. They also heard a bluesy singer from Austin who was soon to move to the Bay Area and become a major force in contemporary music: Janis Joplin.

David left Southern Pacific and through 1964 partnered and toured with fellow folkie and guitarist Michaela Conga in a band dubbed simply David and Michaela. They had an opportunity to record a demo for Elektra Records, but producer Paul Rothchild (later to work with the Paul Butterfield Blues Band, the Doors, and Janis Joplin, among others) passed, telling them the folk-rock sound was on the verge of extinction. CBS Records, however, took a chance and brought them into the studio on February 8, 1964, coincidentally the night before the Beatles' first historic appearance on the Ed Sullivan Show. Neither David nor Michaela were given a copy.

After parting ways with Michaela, David returned to San Francisco and moved in with Paul Kantner and some others. The exact timeline is hazy, but music historian extraordinaire Joel Selvin maintains that David was arrested during the summer of 1965, when he made an illegal left turn and the police officer observed him stashing a small baggie containing less than an ounce of grass under the front seat. No doubt the length of David's hair ("I looked more like an Italian fisherman"), considered somehow subversive by law enforcement in that era, was sufficient to raise suspicion. With the charge still pending, he cut his hair and moved to the Homestead Valley region of Marin County, accompanied by Kantner. He found a job with a freight company, and when not working would "...come home, smoke dope, as much as I could, get out my twelve-string and sing Beatles songs. I learned all the Beatles songs and sang them to the San Rafael Bridge till I fell asleep. And then, I'd do the same thing the next day." He and Kantner were renting a house located above the bridge in San Quentin Village, associating with acquaintances who were similarly disenchanted with the materialism and regimentation of "straight" society. One was a pot dealer who had been busted and offered a deal if he wore a wire in order to entrap fellow users of the noble weed. He asked David to sell him some pot, but David told him he only had some seeds and stems but said he would split them with his "friend". The dealer offered him ten dollars. David said he could have the stash for free, but the buyer insisted on giving him a five. At that point, David was arrested and carted off to the San Rafael jail for a month, unable to post bail. While there, he was visited by Kantner, who slipped him a joint. Before leaving, Kantner said he was joining a band to be called Jefferson Airplane. When the police realized no one was going to bail David out, they released him on his own recognizance. More than fifty year later, he recalled, "I was already talking to John Cipollina and Jimmy Murray about...forming a band with Dino Valenti, who apparently wanted a band, but he couldn't stay out of jail." Dino, who was arrested for pot possession on more than one occasion, ended up spending time not only in municipal jails but also the state prison system, an experience that was to later be the subject of track by Quicksilver.

Temporarily free, David no longer had a job or even a guitar and had to stay with any friends who had a floor for him to sleep on. The trial date for his first arrest was coming up, and he had ten days to turn himself in. He ended up being sentenced to two months in the San Bruno lockup. John Cipollina said he and his friend Jim Murray needed a bass player and would hold that spot open for him, although David had never played the instrument before. When he got out of jail, John, who was living in a 1954 Plymouth on Mount Tamalpais, gave him an old bass he had in his trunk. Gary Duncan eventually demonstrated basic bass patterns for him, which David easily picked up to become one of the most solid players of the instrument in the entire Bay Area.

JOHN

"John was such a unique player, and he was just a really sweet guy, really wonderful person, who would talk to anybody, didn't really think that much about himself..."

David Freiberg, 2019

Early in life, John Cipollina, one of the most incomparable guitarists of the classic rock era, began as a classical pianist. This is not surprising, considering the fact that his stepmother, Evelyn, was a concert pianist. (She later gave lessons to David Freiberg.) He was born John Holland Mallet III (along with his twin sister, Manuela) in Berkeley, California, on August 24, 1943, and adopted by the Cipollinas, a close-knit family which later included another daughter (Antonia) and son (Mario, destined to join Huey Lewis & The News). On his twelfth birthday John's father, Gino, gave him his first guitar. (The Cipollinas were very supportive of John's career choice, going so far as to decorate their house with posters from Quicksilver concerts and often have the band join them for dinner.) In 1959, John assembled a band known as the Penetrators, followed by the Deacons, who stayed together until 1963. The possibility of him one day performing Beethoven sonatas at Carnegie Hall vanished. "We played '50s rock 'n' roll stuff," he recalled in 1985. "Here in San Francisco, there was an unwritten law that once you turned eighteen you stopped playing rock 'n' roll…I was still having fun playing rock 'n' roll and all my friends had gone into folk music. Then the circle came around to folk-rock, and that is when I met David Freiberg…Jim Murray, who I had been palling around with since 1963 or so, turned me onto Freiberg and the three of us started playing together…Dino was the one who got us all together in 1964. Dino had a manager (Tom Donahue), had written hit songs and had a following. Then Dino decided not to be a folk singer anymore. So he hired me to play guitar and Murray to play bass, and we were going to get some other people. We began rehearsing, and Dino got flung into jail on a dope charge. So, me and Murray hung out with David Freiberg. Dino had all these great ideas like having us all wear weird outfits and being lowered onto the stage by wire and playing with cordless guitars and all kinds of things. Dino was really ahead of his time." Dino also told John they would have girls dressed like Native Americans, in short skirts, playing tambourines with their jingle-jangle sound produced by silver dollars. John remembered, "…I'm sitting there going, 'This guy is gonna happen and we're gonna set the world on fire.' I was recommended to Dino, probably because I was the only guy playing an electric guitar, let alone lead, at the time…We talked about rehearsing and planned to rehearse the next night, but it never happened." Dino was arrested for possession, busted again two days after he was released, and then spent nearly the next two years in prison.

In mid-1965, The Charlatans, a Bay Area band formed in the fall of 1964, migrated 500 miles north to Nevada's Virginia City, basically a ghost town, and became the house band at the Red Dog Saloon in the recently remodeled Comstock Hotel. Their lead guitarist, Mike Wilhelm, was busted for pot possession, and when John heard the news, figuring with Dino incarcerated he had nothing to lose, asked the band if they needed a replacement. Unfortunately, his timing was off, as Wilhelm had already been bailed out.

John, along with Jim and David, linked up with Casey Sonoban, a jazz drummer and photographer, and another guitarist, Alexander "Skip" Spence. David proved to be a better bass player than Jim, who switched to harmonica and guitar. Both he and David shared vocal chores. During the autumn of 1965, the unnamed band was able to rehearse at the Matrix, a small club owned by Jefferson

Airplane singer Marty Balin, who loaned them some equipment and required that they perform for the public at least once a month. It wasn't long before Balin asked Spence to audition for the drum seat in the Airplane. Spence's only experience with percussion was rattling the snare in his high school's marching band, but as Balin told journalist Ralph J. Gleason, "I'm very struck by images of people. And I saw him and I said, 'That's my drummer.'" When Spence insisted he only played guitar and sang, Balin told him, "Why don't you get some sticks and work with them, you know? You'd be a great drummer, I can tell...Play for a week and see what happens. If you can play in a week, you can play in our group." The future Quicksilver Messenger Service suddenly found themselves without a drummer. (Spence played on the first Airplane album, released in 1966, and went on to form Moby Grape and record a solo album, *Oar*, in 1969. Now regarded as a classic in some circles, it was a commercial flop. He died homeless thirty years later, addicted to cocaine and heroin.) The band, still without a name, also found themselves without a drummer when Sonoban elected to devote more time to his photography. "He didn't take it seriously," Freiberg said of Sonoban's decision. "We did. We assumed it was going to happen for us. We were confident for some reason."

To make amends for talking Spence into joining the Airplane, Balin suggested Greg Elmore as a candidate to fill the recently vacant drummer's seat. Elmore and his guitarist friend Gary Duncan had been in an outfit called the Brogues and recorded two singles ("Someday"/"But Now I Find" and "Don't Shoot Me Down"/"I Ain't No Miracle Worker") for the small label Challenge Records before the group folded. They were currently crashing in the North Beach basement of Chris Brooks, something of a den mother for San Francisco bands, and hoping to find work playing in a bar band. Brooks introduced them to John one night in October at Longshoremen's Hall, where an organization known as The Family Dog was staging a concert by Jefferson Airplane and the Charlatans dubbed "A Tribute to Dr. Strange." Two nights later, Greg and Gary were jamming with him, David, and Jim on Bo Diddley's "Mona." John recalled that his new acquaintances were, like many young men, living in San Francisco "to dodge the draft." Although John, David, and Jim were living in Marin County, the trio ended up relocating to the city and moving in with the two new band members when the clutch on John's ancient Plymouth gave out and they no longer had a way to commute. With David recently remarried (his bride known simply as Girl Freiberg because she was the only girl in a family with five brothers), and Gary and his girlfriend Shelley about to be, Brooks' basement accommodations on Water Street were becoming quite crowded. Even so, the band rehearsed and began to put together a set list comprised mainly of such blues standards as "Smokestack Lightning," "Back Door Man," and "Who Do You Love?" They rehearsed at the Matrix in September and performed there in November, calling themselves the Vulcans. Another name suggested was Cosmic Crystal Set before the astrological chart provided them with Quicksilver Messenger Service. "Jim Murray and David Freiberg came up with the name," said John. "Me and Freiberg were born on the same day (August 24) and Gary and Greg were born the same day (September 4). We were all Virgos, and Murray was Gemini. And Virgos and Geminis were all ruled by the planet Mercury. Another name for Mercury is Quicksilver. Quicksilver is the messenger of the gods, and Virgo is the servant. So Freiberg says, 'Oh, Quicksilver Messenger Service.'" Asked on one occasion who suggested the name, Freiberg said, "Well, of course I think it was mine. Jim Murray thought it was his, but we were talking together when we came up with it, so I assume it was probably both of ours.

Although I'm sure I was the one who thought of it. As I'm sure he probably is, you know? It seemed like too long and complicated a name, so we kept trying to call it something else, and every time we did, our equipment would blow up or something, so we just said OK. And everybody was using fairly complicated names anyway—Jefferson Airplane, Big Brother and the Holding Company. It seemed to fit the time. I don't think it'd work anymore, but one never knows."

The exact dates and sequence of events will, like much of Quicksilver's early history, be forever obscured by the mists of time, with the recollections of several sources contradicting one another, but no one disputes that the band's first recording was a rock version of "The Star Spangled Banner," used to introduce performances by The Committee, a group of improvisational comics specializing in subversive material. The late Howard Hesseman, who would become a household name in 1978 as rock radio disc jockey Dr. Johnny Fever in the popular sitcom *WKRP in Cincinnati*, was a member of the troupe and paid Quicksilver two-hundred dollars and two ounces of marijuana for the track. The Committee had been using the familiar version by Kate Smith, which while perversely amusing given the context, was not emblematic of the current era. Hesseman and his associates were so knocked out by the recording that the band was hired to play for The Committee's annual holiday bash on Christmas Eve, held in a lodge at Muir Beach. "We played, I think, five sets and got paid $150," John recalled. Up until then we had been playing for nothing. We were amazed that they were paying us to do it." They made their public debut as Quicksilver the following month, returning to the lodge on January 15. One of the attendees happened to be Ambrose Hollingworth, an older "hippie" originally from Chicago, who operated a school of psychic magic in Petaluma and would later write an occasional astrology column for early issues of Rolling Stone, had money and was sufficiently impressed that he offered his services as manager. He also advanced them a thousand dollars to upgrade their equipment, including a PA system, In 1985, John told Goldmine magazine that Alan Myerson (whom he misidentified as Myers), an attorney who had founded and directed The Committee, "backed us initially with, I think, $2,000. We had this deal with him that he made ten percent of what we made and at that time we weren't making anything, so he was worried about his money." The band eventually paid Myerson back "and then we broke the contract," John continued, "because it was a silly deal to begin with." Although Hollingworth handled Quicksilver's affairs for several months, Myers was responsible for introducing the band to the legendary concert promoter Bill Graham, who had opened the hallowed Fillmore Auditorium in November.

The infusion of cash enabled John to have his car repaired and the band to move out of Chris Brooks' basement and into one of four beached houseboats in nearby Larkspur, a swampy area in the hills of Mill Valley, populated by innumerable noisy ducks. The scenery was made more appealing by the presence of majestic Mount Tamalpais, where John had lived in his car, and David Crosby would later immortalize in his 1971 song "Tamalpais High (At About 3)." Through John's realtor father they were able to rent their new furnished digs for one hundred dollars a month, accessible by crossing a boardwalk that tended to be covered by a thin coat of ice in winter. To keep the wood burning stove stoked on chilly nights, slats from neighboring boardwalks were pillaged.

Providentially, one of the band's Larkspur neighbors was Dan Healy, a longtime friend of John and later the soundman for the Grateful Dead. Recalling his early days with Quicksilver, he told author Sandy Troy, "You couldn't avoid hearing them play. They would be going on all day and night. I got to know these guys. Since I worked in recording studios I knew about sound so I went to a gig with them once, the third or fourth gig ever put on in the old Fillmore...I remember going to the gig and being really prepared, because I had been hanging out with these people and had a reasonable idea of what their music was going to sound like." Healy was "appalled" by the audio quality of the band's performance and elected to do something about it. "We went and rented from this sound company in San Francisco just about all the sound equipment they had. We took the equipment to a gig one night and stacked it up all over the place." Grateful Dead manager Rock Scully would later remark that Healy did "amazing things for Quicksilver."

*

GREG

"The guy Paul with the group Blue Cheer—used to be with the Oxford Circle—excellent heavy rock drummer. I like Greg with Quicksilver, he's in the same bag. Not quite as flashy as Paul, but he's heavy."

Spencer Dryden, Jefferson Airplane drummer,
to Ralph J. Gleason, 1969

Not much is known about Greg Elmore, the only member of Quicksilver to play on every album the band recorded from 1967 to the reunion of the original lineup in 1975. (He was also the only member this author had the opportunity to speak with, though briefly, more than fifty years ago.) Born at California's Coronado Naval Air Station on September 4, 1946, and due to his family's military lifestyle, lived in Oklahoma, Washington, Nebraska, and Arizona. He began playing drums in the sixth grade and was in his high school's marching band. After studying liberal arts in junior college, he joined a surf group called Pendulum before co-founding the Brogues with Gary Duncan in 1965. After recording their pair of unsuccessful singles ("Someday" was, however, a minor hit in central California), and with Southern California pop groups the proverbial dime-a-dozen, they decided to try their luck in San Francisco. In her 2002 memoir, Gary's former wife Shelley revealed that Greg was transformed from being generally good natured to moody and increasingly withdrawn, allegedly after a bad experience with the hallucinatory drug LSD (lysergic acid diethylamide), known on the street as simply acid. The crystalline drug was first synthesized in Switzerland by a Dr. Albert Hoffman, who accidentally ingested it five years later and reported it put him "in a dream-like state, with eyes closed" and that he "perceived an uninterrupted stream of fantastic pictures, extraordinary shapes with intense, kaleidoscopic play of colors." Although a second "trip" initially resulted in feelings of paranoia, the pleasant sensations took over and he became convinced it could be utilized as a psychiatric treatment. Indeed, it was later used to study schizophrenia, and the U.S. military experimented with it as a nefarious form of mind control. As Dr. Hoffman discovered, LSD did not affect everyone who tried it the same way, no doubt due largely to one's brain chemistry and existing personality. Nor was an individual's reaction to the drug the same every time. At first a legal substance, though potentially more harmful than the already-banned marijuana (now legal in half of the United States, containing medicinal properties and far less physically damaging than alcohol), the government quickly outlawed it in 1966 once its use by the general public—particularly young musicians who found it expanded the horizons of their creativity—became known. "We took a lot of drugs," Gary admitted. "It sounds a little trite, but drugs had a lot to do with it. Weed, LSD, speed, DMT; you name it, we took it and played music on it. I'm not advocating drug use; it's just a fact."

In a 1969 article by an unidentified journalist, Greg was described as "...very, very quiet. He is quiet in the way thoughtful people are quiet, not an unfriendly quiet, nor a bored quiet, a respectful-for-silence kind of quiet." It's difficult to believe Elmore was drug-addled by the time I met him, and it's difficult to believe he could have been as forceful and technically sharp at the Quicksilver shows I was fortunate to see. As veteran rock journalist and Quicksilver historian Dave Thompson remarked in his 2015 liner notes regarding a 1967 performance, "Has there ever been a rhythm section to match David Freiberg and Greg Elmore, in the annals of rock, anyway? Psychic syncopation, they could have been backing up the most electric funk onstage at the Apollo; they could have been James Brown's most famous Flames. That's how good they were, and in any other band, maybe they were the sound to which most ears would have gravitated." Remembered Gary, "The folk guys didn't know how to get a groove going. One of the reasons we did so well at first is Greg was such a good drummer. He was loud." In a rare interview, Greg would remark, "We'd just take a song and beat the shit out of it."

Before dropping out of sight, Greg went on to play in Terry & The Pirates (1981-89), one of John's many post-Quicksilver bands, and was interviewed for a 1991 video tribute to John. A lawsuit over ownership of the name Quicksilver Messenger Service reportedly ruined his friendship with Gary.

*

JIM

"He thought the idea of going into a recording studio and staying there for days just wasn't his idea of fun."

John Cipollina, 1985

Rhythm guitarist, harmonica player and singer Jim Murray, born on May 30, 1942, was the Pete Best of Quicksilver, out of the band when they were on the threshold of true success. Unlike the ill-fated Beatle, he quit voluntarily, roughly around September 1967. Some sources maintain he was forced out, though he was never replaced. The conventional line is that he lacked ambition, wanted to study the sitar after hearing Ravi Shankar at the Monterey Pop Festival, and moved to Hawaii to work on boats. Jim, his bushy blond hair reminiscent of Brian Jones of the Rolling Stones or Michael Clarke of the Byrds, can be seen performing "Dino's Song"—listed as "All I Ever Wanted To Do (Was Love You)"—in an outtake from the Monterey film released on DVD by The Criterion Collection in 2002. The excerpt is also on the DVD compilation of the band's videos included in the *Quicksilver Anthology Box 1966-1970* released by Cleopatra Records in 2011. Presumably Jim's aversion to the often tedious process of working in the studio was a result of participating in early demo sessions at Pacific High Studios in San Francisco, Hollywood's Continental Sounds Studios, and the recording of two tracks ("Babe, I'm Gonna Leave You," "Codine") the band contributed to *Revolution*, filmmaker Jack O'Connell's documentary of the hippie lifestyle circa 1967. Not released until 1968, it featured dark, shaky footage of the band performing live in a San Francisco nightclub during the summer of '67, Jim and David glimpsed only briefly. Jim was back on the mainland by 1970 and performed intermittently with Copperhead, another of John's bands after leaving

Quicksilver. Copperhead recorded an album for Columbia in 1973, but Jim was not among the players. He passed away in March of 2013 at the age of 70.

*

GARY

"You didn't realize how good Gary was on guitar because John was so flashy and charismatic. Gary's solos were note-perfect."

John Goddard, former owner of Village Music in Mill Valley, 2019

Gary was born Eugene Duncan, Jr., in San Diego on September 4, 1946. Adopted at birth, he was renamed Gary Grubb and spent his youth in Ceres, California, running away from home in 1961 at the age of fifteen and playing bass in a Las Vegas combo known variously as the Make-Believers or the Soul Mates. He earned enough to buy a convertible as well as pot, which landed him in jail for a little more than a year. It is not clear if he was drafted or enlisted, but Gary spent parts of 1962 and 1963 in Vietnam, a fact not generally known. "I was a sniper for the 75th Airborne…I got back right before Kennedy was assassinated…I never talked to anybody about it. That wasn't a real popular subject in San Francisco…I wouldn't have been allowed in the band." Back in California he became lead guitarist for a band called the Ratz. There's no evidence the Ratz ever made a record, but they were able to land gigs as an opening act for the Byrds and the Rolling Stones. In 1965 Gary, calling himself Gary Cole, met Greg Elmore in Merced, California. (After discovering his birth certificate, Gary changed his surname a final time to that of his birth father.) They began sharing an apartment, formed The Brogues (inspired either by the Irish dialect or a type of Irish shoe leather), called their sound "American music with British accents", and became the first members of Quicksilver to see the inside of a recording studio. When their two singles went nowhere nationally, they spent approximately five minutes that September contemplating a move to San Francisco. The following month they were there. "Since I was about thirteen I had been coming up to San Francisco and hanging out in North Beach, taking speed, drinking a lot, smoking pot," Gary recalled. He and John combined to become the most explosive, adventurous guitarists of the Bay Area, incorporating their mutual love of the blues, rock, psychedelia, and jazz. "The Quicksilver, you know," observed Jefferson Airplane bassist Jack Casady, "if you listen to Gary, you can tell he's listening to jazz." In the opinion of retired Mill Valley record store owner John Goddard, who married John's twin sister, heard the original lineup more than one hundred times. "They were the best of all the San Francisco bands," he said. "When Quicksilver was on, they could blow the doors off the Dead and the Airplane. And when they were off, they were still better than most bands." One reason for their excellence was the band's communal living situation. In Gary's words, "We played together a lot because we all lived together…It is amazing looking back on it, but at the time it was just being young and having fun and playing in a band and playing a lot of shows. The only band we were close to was the

Grateful Dead. We knew everybody. Of course because we were on the same bill with everyone at one time or another, but we actually hung out with the Dead quite a bit before everyone got record deals and started going out on the road."

While the Grateful Dead had a more extensive and varied repertoire—largely because they outlasted nearly all of their contemporaries for an astounding two decades—Quicksilver's affinity for jazz-like improvisation rendered the similarities of their sets immaterial. "We played a lot of the same songs because we hadn't worn them out yet," Gary explained. "They still had places to go…We never had set lists. We didn't actually know what we were going to play. We just got real stoned and went on the stage and let it happen the way it happened. We had our own arrangements and had open places where we would just wail...just playing one tune for three or four hours was nothing. That was no big deal whatsoever. At rehearsals we'd sit there and play for seven, eight hours straight, ten hours. We'd play 'til we just fall over and the hands were bleeding." Gary's former wife, Shelley, revealed that her husband would more often than not have a bruised thigh from banging a tambourine against his leg in concert, as can be seen in footage of the band filmed at the Monterey Pop Festival. Surprisingly, he only sang and rattled the tambourine in the earliest days of the band, contributing little guitar work although he was more skilled and imaginative than Jim. That would soon change, his emphatic slash-and-burn style a dramatic contrast to John's quivering waves of sound. "In the beginning it was just John," Gary recalled. "I was mostly the singer when the band started. Then our manager heard me playing one day and said, 'Hey, you play guitar. We can have two guitars.' John and I were opposite types of player, so we fitted together well because we didn't sound the same." Sound engineer Dan Healy observed, "Gary is more of an on-beat player. John's a backbeat player…John heard things more like string sections from Mars."

Gary was on all but one of Quicksilver's studio albums (quitting from December 1968 to December 1969) and kept the band's name alive with a series of albums until 2010, sometimes with the assistance of Dino and David. "Gary was the engine of Quicksilver," David said. Although Gary would concede that "live shows were our bread and butter", he was said to be the most driven and disciplined member of the original lineup when they began making records. Describing the difference between performing live and recording, he told the Village Voice: "Playing something in a studio means playing for two months. Playing live, a song changes in performance. In a studio, you attack things intellectually; onstage it's all emotion."

*

NICKY

England's Nicky Hopkins was, without question, the most highly acclaimed—and busiest—keyboard artist of the classic rock era. It would almost be easier to list the bands that *didn't* avail themselves of his services. Some of the most prominent ones that did include the Who, the Kinks, the Rolling Stones, the Yardbirds, the Steve Miller Band, Jefferson Airplane, and of course, the Beatles. He was born in a suburb of London on February 24, 1944, and began playing the piano at the age of three. Before he was twenty he had been a member of bands led by Screaming Lord Sutch and Cyril Davies, but poor health that would plague him throughout his life usually prevented him from doing much touring. As a result, he became one of the most in-demand session musicians in England.

In 1966 he recorded an instrumental album of mostly covers ("Yesterday," "Satisfaction," "Goldfinger," "Love Letters"), *The Revolutionary Piano of Nicky Hopkins*, accompanied by a full orchestra. The only standout track was his "Jenni." Two years later, he joined the now-forgotten band Sweet Thursday, who never performed live and recorded but one album. Before that was even released he had begun working somewhat steadily with former Yardbird Jeff Beck, playing piano on four tracks of the landmark *Truth* and becoming a full-fledged member of the group—with band mates Rod Stewart and Ron Wood—for a second album, 1969's *Beck-Ola*. The band's tour of the United States prior to that record included four nights at the Fillmore West in December 1968. It was Nicky's first time in California, and he was deeply affected by the experience, attracted especially to the beauty of Mill Valley, just north of San Francisco. He spent some time among the musical community and was enchanted by David Freiberg's young wife Julia (then known as Girl), who was the inspiration for Nicky's instrumental "Girl from Mill Valley," recorded in early April for *Beck-Ola*. Although he originally claimed the song was "about nobody," when the truth eventually leaked out he was disappointed because he had intended to tell Julia himself. "Nicky really liked me and I liked him," she told Nicky's biographer Julian Dawson. "He was a decent, sensitive guy but very innocent and naïve; he'd had a very sheltered life, but he was sweet and I could tell he had a big crush on me." When Rolling Stone got around to reviewing *Beck-Ola* in August, "Girl from Mill Valley" was given a mixed reception: "There's a change of pace with 'Girl from Mill Valley—a lovely, wistful gospel tune written by Hopkins, which toward the end teeters unfortunately on the edge of Mancini-land. The addition of a vocal part would have made it even better."

The Jeff Beck Group's third tour of the U.S. was also its last. After a disastrous show at the Fillmore East in May 1969, Beck returned to England without telling the rest of the band. Nicky opted to return to the West Coast, where Jefferson Airplane recruited him to play on their outstanding *Volunteers* album, which they had started recording in March. "Nicky was great, totally professional," said bassist Jack Casady. "He was a rather quiet fellow, but not quiet in his playing. Musically, he connected well and I enjoyed his playing. When Grace (Slick) and Paul (Kantner) primarily wanted to have Nicky to broaden the sound on the tracks a bit, and to add the dynamics of the piano, he was able to do beautiful things." Nicky sat in with the Airplane at the legendary Woodstock Festival, then a member of Quicksilver and the only member of the band to be at the historic event.

Shortly after working with the Airplane, he recorded extensively with the Steve Miller Band. Miller was so knocked out by

Nicky's piano on "Baby's House" (a nine-minute cut on *Your Saving Grace*) that he gave him a co-writing credit. Later that year, Nicky said that *Your Saving Grace* was "one of the most interesting and enjoyable albums I've ever done." "We played a few gigs in San Francisco," Miller recalled, "but he never really came on the road with us, because he was really not in good shape. I remember being surprised that he came over (to America), because he'd had so many health problems. We called him 'The Mummy' because he was so thin, but we were still disappointed when he joined Quicksilver."

Quicksilver had tried continuing as a trio in Gary's absence, but were struggling and in need of a replacement. Manager Ron Polte remembered, "We were looking for six months or more and auditioned a few people, but no one fit. Nicky was so versatile, it was perfect. His playing on *Beggars Banquet* (the Rolling Stones' 1968 classic) had flipped us all out and I really wanted to meet the guy." Nicky was still recording with Miller when "John and David came up to see me and asked if I'd stay on after Steve's album to do some work" on the album *Shady Grove*. John, who was to become one of Nicky's closest and most enduring friends, was as happily stunned as David and Greg by the keyboard wizard's addition to the track "Joseph's Coat." "He listened to it once, making a few notes on a piece of paper and then went straight over to the piano, taped his jottings in front of him and played it first take! It was just astonishing. So he joined the group and we all felt a real resurgence." "By this time," Nicky said, "I was beginning to dread returning to England, and by the time the Quicksilver album was finished, I had joined the group and decided to stay." Today *Shady Grove* is best remembered for his amazing composition "Edward, (The Mad Shirt Grinder)."

Nicky remained with Quicksilver through two additional albums (*Just For Love*, *What About Me*) leaving in 1970 and going on to work with such artists as Badfinger, Donovan, John Lennon, Carly Simon, George Harrison, Joe Cocker, and dozens more. He recorded two solo albums for CBS—*The Tin Man Was A Dreamer*

(1973) and the unreleased *The Long Journey Home* (1974)—and one for Mercury, 1975's *No More Changes*. Despite health issues he persevered, appearing on albums by—among many others—Jerry Garcia, Graham Parker, Art Garfunkel, Pure Prairie League, Paul McCartney, old cronies Rod Stewart and Ron Wood, and with John and Greg in Terry & the Pirates. "I loved playing with Nicky and hadn't worked with him since our days together in Quicksilver Messenger Service," Greg said in reference to a stint with Terry & the Pirates in 1982, "and this short tour was bound to be an adventure of a lifetime and I wasn't about to miss out on it for anything." Nicky died in Nashville, succumbing to Crohn's disease on September 6, 1994, at the age of fifty.

*

1966-67

"These people are all adults, and seriously intent on perfecting good rock as an art. Another of the more established units is Quicksilver Messenger Service. They are a good dance band. No recorded efforts have appeared yet, perhaps as the group has until recently been void of any substantial number of original compositions. Their best numbers are 'Codeine,' Hamilton Camp's 'Pride of Man,' 'Mona,' and 'Smokestack Lightning.'"

Crawdaddy, October 20, 1966

The presence of the United States military in Vietnam grew to nearly 400,000 during 1966. At home, the National Association of Broadcasters ordered disc jockeys to make sure records did not contain any obscene material or hidden messages. Bill Russell of basketball's Boston Celtics became the first Black coach of a professional sports team in history. The Traffic Safety Act requiring car safety standards was signed into law the same year as consumer advocate Ralph Nader reported that General Motors' Corvair was dangerous. The first successful artificial heart transplant took place in Texas.

Life observes no clock or calendar, and if the Fifties ended with the assassination of President Kennedy on November 22, 1963, and the Beatles' first visit to the United States on February 7, 1964, launched the Sixties, a reasonably solid case can be made for citing 1966 as the year the classic rock era truly began. Twenty of the fifty best-selling albums of 1966 were either rock or pop, eight of them ranking among the top one hundred of the decade: *Revolver* and *Yesterday And Today* (The Beatles); *Parsley, Sage, Rosemary And Thyme* and *Sounds of Silence* (Simon & Garfunkel); *Blonde On Blonde* (Bob Dylan); *Pet Sounds* (The Beach Boys); *Aftermath*

(The Rolling Stones); and *If You Can Believe Your Eyes And Ears* (The Mamas & The Papas). It was also the year the Beatles stopped touring, the Beach Boys released "Good Vibrations," Bob Dylan's momentum was curtailed by a motorcycle crash, Grace Slick joined Jefferson Airplane, Cream and the Jimi Hendrix Experience were formed in England, and Buffalo Springfield came together in Los Angeles. At the same time, America's growing involvement in Vietnam resulted in, as Rolling Stone's *Rock Almanac* recalled in 1983, music that "...was now being consciously used as a weapon in what was becoming a cultural war between the young generation and the old establishment."

Archival information regarding Quicksilver's concert history is extensive though neither complete nor accurate. (One lists only one of the two shows I attended, another neither of them.) Following their first official gig as Quicksilver Messenger Service on January 15, the band spent the entire year playing more than eighty shows, all in California and mainly in San Francisco at such now-sacred places as The Avalon Ballroom and especially the Fillmore Auditorium, later renamed the Fillmore West. A Midwestern promoter offered them a September date in Chicago, which never took place. In December they ventured south to play Los Angeles for the first time, which was somewhat surprising. As Richard Goldstein of the Village Voice reported, "San Francisco musicians associate Los Angeles with the evils of studio music. This is probably because almost every group has made the trek south to record. And the music available on record so far is anything but hard rock. But resentment of Los Angeles goes much deeper than the recording studio. The rivalry between Northern and Southern California makes a cold war in pop inevitable. While musicians in Los Angeles deride the sound from up north as 'pretentious and self-conscious' and shudder at the way 'people live like animals up there,' the Northern attitude is best summed up by a member of the Quicksilver Messenger Service who quipped, 'L.A. hurts our eyes.'" So said Gary after witnessing the glittering Sunset Strip after sundown. In recent years seven dates recorded between May and November, have surfaced, taped at the Fillmore, the Matrix, the Avalon, and the I.E.S Hall in San Jose. While these shows are top-heavy with blues standards ("You Don't Love Me," "Hoochie Coochie Man," "Walkin' Blues," etc.), there are several original compositions ("Dino's Song," "Stand By Me," "The Fool," "Gold and Silver") that wouldn't be officially recorded for over a year.

In August, RCA released *Takes Off*, the first album by Jefferson Airplane, including Dino's "Let's Get Together." "All of a sudden," John said, "...when they started recording, they were walking around with long faces. Then the Dead signed, and the same thing happened...they weren't nearly as much fun. And all the groups were being urged to go out on tour, promoting their albums over as much of the country as they could cover, and nobody ever seemed to be playing around town anymore. The scene was breaking up, but we were still around, and we weren't about to sign up and leave the area, so we got all the gigs we could handle. We shared the bill with so many different people, everyone from Howling Wolf to The Doors, but we got more money than any of them, even though we hadn't got an album out or anything. So we stayed around...never did too much travelling, except up and down the state." In another interview, he said, "We developed a bad attitude towards record companies and the like. When record companies called we would just ignore them."

Band manager Ambrose Hollingworth was able to move the Quicksilver family from the Larkspur houseboat—sometimes referred to as a shack—to a two-story house in Mill Valley. The spacious dwelling, which was christened the Creek House, rented for two-hundred dollars a month, double what they had been paying, but frequent bookings easily covered the cost. The band also borrowed a used panel van from a friend for transporting their equipment, which included John's distinctive ten-foot high Fender rig consisting of a solid state amplifier on the bottom, a tube amp on top. In addition, he attached horn-shaped extensions that tripled the audio output. (This imposing tower was later donated to the Rock & Roll Hall of Fame.) John was skilled at building guitars and favored thin gauge strings which, when played using a wang bar, produced his characteristic trembling tone. It also put the instrument out of tune, which he rectified when the strings were manipulated and he, as David remembered, "...pulled" it into tune. "And he used a couple of finger picks, a thumb pick and a finger pick, and some of the times he would just be rubbing the strings so it would just make strange noises with the wah-wah pedal. And he designed pick guards for his guitar so they looked like batwings." John's piercing, tremulous style was to have a significant impact on the late Tom Verlaine, co-founder of the Seventies band Television.

When Hollingworth was confined to a wheelchair following an auto accident, management of the band passed to Ron Polte, who had operated a folk den in Chicago with his brother Frank and moved to San Francisco to avoid some legal entanglements and start life anew. Nick Gravenites, also a native of Chicago—and future member of the Electric Flag—recommended Polte to Hollingworth. (Gravenites himself would soon figure prominently in the Quicksilver saga.)

It fell to Polte to seek yet another location—the fourth—for the band to live and rehearse in. The Creek House was frequently a destination for runaway teens, particulary girls, and the Mill Valley police usually went looking for them there, often breaking the musical spell Quicksilver was in the process of conjuring during their marathon practices. "It was really ridiculous," David recalled. Polte found a rundown dairy farm (sometimes referred to as a ranch) in Olema, on the western fringe of Marin County. The rent was a mere eighty-five dollars a month, which was easily affordable considering they could play a three-night stand at the Fillmore for up to a thousand dollars. And they appeared there more than two dozen times in 1966 alone. Their new manager also bought used Dodge Darts at auction for each member of the band. The Quicksilver family cleaned up the property enough to make it reasonably livable, hired a roadie named Greg Collins, and moved in, rehearsing in the main house for at least four nights a week. John somehow acquired a timber wolf pup, which he named Wolf, who refused to be housebroken and was a nuisance to everyone but John.

Around this time, Polte convinced the band to at least temporarily set aside their aversion to recording and cut some tracks. The band agreed to a late night session at a small San Francisco studio ordinarily used for making radio commercials, but to date these historical first attempts have never been released. It would be a year before anyone outside California could hear what Quicksilver sounded like.

The summer of 1966 was, in the estimation of many who were there, the true Summer of Love, not 1967, the media's Summer of Love. Several Bay Area bands would congregate in the open country of Marin County for endless jam sessions. "Everything was just super groovy," Jerry Garcia of the Dead would recall nearly a decade later. "It was a model of how things could be really good. All that was the firming up of the whole social world of rock and roll around here." (During a Thanksgiving dinner held at the Grateful Dead's house in the Haight/Ashbury neighborhood, attended by every member of Jefferson Airplane and Quicksilver, Dead bassist Phil Lesh gave a toast: "These *are* the good old days.")

A young woman arrived at the ranch one day and announced that Dino instructed her to stay there until he was released from jail the following week. She was originally from Los Angeles and claimed to have designed the bell bottom jeans worn by Sonny and Cher. Although she was supposedly Dino's girlfriend, she—in the spirit of the times—latched onto Jim until Dino was free.

When Dino showed up, wearing beads, carrying a wooden flute, and accompanied by a Great Dane named Mando, he took one look at short-haired Ron Polte and asked who he was. When Polte replied that he was the band's manager, Dino told him he didn't look like a manager, and walked off. He took it upon himself to put his girlfriend in charge of Quicksilver's communal savings, which did not go over well with Shelley Duncan or Geri Elmore, Greg's wife, who had to plead for gas and cigarette money. Dino's girlfriend said that it was fine with Jim and David, but Dino told her the cash belonged to everyone.

One night the ranch was raided by "Indians" wearing feathered headdresses, their faces smeared with war paint. On horseback they attacked the main house with smoke bombs and firecrackers. The "settlers" soon recognized the warriors as members of the Grateful Dead, riding over from their own ranch, an abandoned summer camp in Lagunitas. The musicians had a good laugh and smoked a peace pipe filled, naturally, with pot. "That was fun and all," David said more than fifteen years later, "but we were determined to get them back for their raid on our dope, and we developed this great plan. They were scheduled to play a show at the Fillmore with the Airplane a couple of nights later, so we decided to raid their show dressed as cowboys, with cap guns, masks, and all. We were going to tie them to their amplifiers, play 'Kaw-Liga Was a Wooden Indian' with their instruments and then split. We had Bill Graham's cooperation and even rehearsed the song." Time was not on Quicksilver's side. The Airplane's performance was running late, which necessitated a temporary postponement. The band was seen putting the fake guns back into their equipment van, and the police were called. The officers were already in the area to deal with a riot following the shooting of a young black thief. "All of a sudden the front door opened and a .357 magnum came in," said David. "The cops ripped us out of the truck and searched it thoroughly. They busted us and I ended up spending the night in jail, with a bunch of really pissed-off black guys who were calling me a 'blue-eyed devil.' We never did get to raid the Dead. With my luck it would've ended the same way if we had." Because he had gone off for a cup of coffee with John instead of staying with the van, Dino avoided being tossed in the slammer yet again. He was not officially a member of the band, though he would occasionally sit in; he wouldn't play the Fillmore as a solo act until February, when Quicksilver was billed along with Jefferson Airplane for three nights.

For several reasons, it became apparent that the band's adventures in Olema had to end. Not only were Wolf and Mando chasing neighbors' horses and cows, farmers in the area accused the canines of killing sheep. Straight society decided to force the Quicksilver family out. "There was somebody that ran the stables who wanted to take over the farm," David said. "They'd do things like slaughter a cow right outside our house. It was kind of insane. Murray was living in a chicken coop." Sanitation workers refused to pick up the ranch's garbage, the service station would not sell them gas, store clerks and restaurant servers ignored them. An armed group of citizens finally threatened violence if major changes weren't made. The sensible solution was to move out, especially since, as David recalled, "We realized any time we had a gig we'd have to pile all the stuff in this Volkswagon bus and drive all the way to the city, and then drive all the way back out there again. And all our gigs were at like the Fillmore, the Avalon…The audiences got huge. I remember driving up to the Avalon and seeing the line up and down the block."

Back in San Francisco, David, Gary, Greg and their wives (as well as roadie Collins) moved into two apartments in a large four-story house, where David did most of the cooking. John and Jim shared a house nearby. The band closed out 1966 with a New Year's Eve bash at the Fillmore that ended with them joining a monumental jam session by members of the Grateful Dead, the Jefferson Airplane, and Big Brother & the Holding Company. By the time it was over, the sun was coming up. Incredibly, Quicksilver was able to recover sufficiently to play a "Giant Freak Out" at the Winterland Auditorium, located two blocks from the Fillmore, the next night.

Even without any recorded evidence, the band, which one scribe said had "a punk cowboy image", had managed to become one of the top draws in the city by the end of 1966. As music historian Mikal Gilmore wrote in 2008, "…the band on its best nights was the fiercest of any of the San Francisco bands, featuring long-ranging suites and mesmeric instrumental passages, driven by John Cipollina's fleet and sinuous guitar lines and Greg Elmore's impelling drum thrusts."

"If you examine San Francisco closely, you'll find major changes taking place in almost every aspect of city life. New attitudes toward jobs, education, toward entertainment and the arts. Basic shifts in the relationships between man and his environment, changes that have affected every facet of that environment, changes that best can be communicated not in words but in music: Big Brother & the Holding Company, Jefferson Airplane, Moby Grape, Steve Miller Blues Band, Country Joe & the Fish, Quicksilver Messenger Service, the Dead.

Crawdaddy, June 1967

Increasing protests against the war in Vietnam included more than 75,000 protesters marching on the Pentagon. Thurgood Marshall became the first Black Supreme Court justice. The number of telephones installed in the United States reached 100 million. Significant oil deposits were discovered in Alaska. The elimination of background noise in audio recordings was made possible by the invention of the Dolby device. Folk rockers Simon & Garfunkel provided music for the soundtrack of *The Graduate.*

In 1967, more than half of the top-selling 100 albums were rock, pop, and rhythm and blues for the first time, eight of them earning Gold Records, a dozen among the best 100 sellers of the decade. It was also the last year movie and Broadway soundtracks and easy listening artists would dominate the upper region of the chart. The times had definitely changed. New artists included Pink Floyd, Procol Harum, and the Bee Gees, whose early albums featured cryptic lyrics and production superior to their disco output in the next decade. The Who mounted their first major US tour. The Byrds fired David Crosby. The Grateful Dead released their first album. Jefferson Airplane's *Surrealistic Pillow* produced the first nationally popular music from San Francisco (#6 album, #22 single "Somebody to Love"). Two Beatles—Paul McCartney and George Harrison—checked out the Bay Area scene. McCartney came in April to meet Jefferson Airplane, especially fellow bass player Jack Casady, whose skill on the instrument he greatly admired. When singer Marty Balin asked what the Beatles were up to, McCartney gave the band a preview of "A Day in the Life." "Imagine," said Balin, "being a little stoned, with McCartney, hearing that for the first time. I about died." Harrison made the trip in August and was less than enamored of the Haight-Ashbury district. "I went there expecting it to be a brilliant place," he recalled, "with gypsy people making groovy art and paintings and carvings in little shops. But it was full of horrible spotty drop-out kids on drugs, and it turned me right off the whole scene. I could only describe it as being like the Bowery: a lot of bums and drop-outs; many of them very young kids who'd dropped acid and come from all over America to this Mecca of LSD."

Had Harrison arrived a year earlier he would have discovered the mellower, more artistic environment he anticipated, but once magazines such as Time and Life and the three national television networks started reporting on the new youth culture emerging in San Francisco, the bloom was off the rose, flower power trampled by commercialism, bus tours, runaways, bad drugs, and violence. It was enough to convince the members of Quicksilver to return to the relative peace of rural Marin County, which they did the same month as Harrison's visit.

As for the Beatles, they released the spellbinding single "Strawberry Fields Forever" and the most influential musical milestone of

1967: *Sgt. Pepper's Lonely Hearts Club Band,* just as the mass media declared that the next three months would be known as the Summer of Love. At the end of the year, they would release *Magical Mystery Tour,* their last album as a harmonious unit.

The positive vibes of the previous year continued for roughly the first half of the new one. "There was incredible optimism in the Haight as 1966 turned into 1967," wrote author and Grateful Dead historian Blair Jackson. "The bands were getting better and more popular; the steady influx of freaks from other parts of the country brought new energy into the scene but still seemed manageable; and increasingly the neighborhood felt like an oasis far away from straight society—a vision of what many felt was a better world in every aspect." "It was a pretty blessed thing that seemed to be happening for a few weeks in 1967," David told *Rolling Stone* in 2018. "Everything was going so right for everybody. Then came all the publicity and all the people coming into Haight-Ashbury and the Gray Line bus tours up and down the street."

Fortuitously, Quicksilver was part of the social landmark festival The Human Be-In, held on the polo fields of Golden Gate Park on January 14. It was an oddly warm day, resulting in a crowd of thousands (estimates vary from 4,500 to and unlikely 20,000) that inspired similar large communal events in New York and Los Angeles later in the year. It would become known as a Gathering of the Tribes, immortalized in David Crosby and Chris Hillman's "Tribal Gathering," recorded by The Byrds in August and released on their January 1968 album *The Notorious Byrd Brothers,* a full year after the Be-In. It was the largest audience Quicksilver Messenger Service had faced, their performance interrupted by a brief power outage. Other bands included the Grateful Dead, Jefferson Airplane, the Sir Douglas Quintet, the Loading Zone, and jazz artists Dizzy Gillespie on trumpet and Charles Lloyd on flute. Another flautist was Dino, who pranced through the masses while poet Alan Ginsberg, author Ken Kesey, and acid promoter Timothy Leary spoke from the stage.

For their last gig of the month, January 26-27, Quicksilver performed outside California for the first time, venturing farther north to the Eagles Auditorium in Seattle, Washington.

The three night stand with Jefferson Airplane at the Fillmore in February, with a solo set by Dino, took place on 3rd, 4th, and 5th of the month. A recording released in 2008 that purports to be from the 6th is, in reality, taken from one or more of the previous three nights because, according to the Fillmore's archives, there was no show on the 6th.

Quicksilver spent the early spring playing no less than fifteen dates in such California locales outside San Francisco as Merced, Santa Clara, Berkeley, San Jose, San Rafael, and Santa Cruz by the end of March. Some of the bands sharing the stage included Buffalo Springfield, Blue Cheer, and Sparrow, soon to be renamed Steppenwolf. Two sets taped at the Matrix on March 19 have been unearthed, as well as some early demos and rehearsal sessions recorded at San Francisco's Pacific High Studios that are available in one configuration or another on several posthumous releases. At this time the band *may* have recorded their contributions to the *Revolution* soundtrack: Buffy Sainte-Marie's "Codine" (spelled "Cod'ne" on her 1964 debut album) and "Babe, I'm Gonna Leave You," more or less a traditional folk number adapted by Erik Darling, though the composing credits are also listed as Darling/Bennett/Bredon. (The most well-known version is a 1969 variation by Led Zeppelin, with Robert Plant and Jimmy Page tacking their names onto Bredon's as composers.) Quicksilver's first commercial efforts remained unheard until May 1968, when both the soundtrack and their own first album were released.

On April 8, the general public was first exposed to Quicksilver on the local television show The Maze, broadcast by KPIX-TV, hosted by San Francisco Chronicle critic Ralph J. Gleason, who in November would launch Rolling Stone magazine with co-founder Jann Wenner. The band lip-synced to Robert Johnson's "Walkin'

Blues" and Hamilton Camp's "Pride of Man," which would much later open their first album. (A familiar photo from the show was most recently used as the front cover of the 2023 *Rare Tracks* compilation from Cleopatra Records.) The show was pre-taped and aired the same day they were playing at the Mount Tamalpais Outdoor Theater with Big Brother & the Holding Company, Sparrow, and the Charlatans.

Before the so-called Summer of Love commenced, Quicksilver's nearly two-dozen live dates included four benefit concerts, two of them promoting anti-war sentiments being voiced by a growing number of citizens of all ages. In addition to the Grateful Dead, Jefferson Airplane, Country Joe and the Fish, Big Brother and the Holding Company, Sopwith Camel, Moby Grape, the Loading Zone, the Steve Miller Blues Band, and Judy Collins, speakers included such activists as Julian Bond, Eldridge Cleaver, Mrs. Martin Luther King, and David Harris, then the husband of Joan Baez. (The other benefits were to protest the arrest of the San Francisco Mime Troupe and in support of HALO, the Haight-Ashbury Legal Organization.) Quicksilver's most overt social commentary was delivered via Hamilton Camp's anti-nuclear anthem "Pride of Man."

On June 16, the opening day of the three-day Monterey International Pop Festival at the Horse Show Arena of the Monterey County Fairgrounds, Quicksilver was performing at a high school graduation dance in Palo Alto, unaware that their fortunes were to undergo a remarkable change the following day.

Monterey, organized by John Phillips of the Mamas and the Papas and their manager, Lou Adler, was the first—and arguably best—rock festival. All of the major San Francisco bands regarded the affair as nothing but crass Hollywood commercialism and declined invitations to perform, even though the bands were appearing free. Eventually, the Grateful Dead, Jefferson Airplane, Big Brother and the Holding Company, Country Joe and the Fish, the Steve Miller Band, Moby Grape, and Quicksilver Messenger Service accepted.

Only the Grateful Dead, Moby Grape, and Quicksilver did not appear in the film shot by D.A. Pennebaker, released in 1969, or the extensive box set of performances released thirty years later. The latter's performance of "Dino's Song" would be made available on DVD in 1997, with David telling the crowd, "That song was written by Dino Valenti." (The managers of all three bands insisted on either financial compensation or control of what film footage could be used.)

The morning prior to their set on Saturday, June 17, Quicksilver joined the Grateful Dead, Jefferson Airplane, Jimi Hendrix, and Eric Burdon and the Animals in a jam session on the Athletic Field of Monterey Peninsula College. "I think the Monterey Pop Festival as an experience was the best for me," Gary recalled years later. "We were there in the company of the biggest music stars in the world, and we got to hang out with them and be one of the crew which was really a 'heady' experience for us. Not to mention getting to see and hear all our heroes. Think about it! What more could a kid with a guitar want?"

Saturday was the longest of the three days, fifteen acts starting with Canned Heat and concluding with Otis Redding's galvanizing set, which no one would have wanted to follow. Quicksilver was sixth on the bill, sandwiched between the Butterfield Blues Band and the Steve Miller Band. "We had a terrible case of stage fright," Gary admitted. "There we were on the stage with some of the biggest names in the music business. We just did our set and got off the stage as soon as we could, and watched the 'Big Guys.'"

Inevitably, representatives of the major record labels came to Monterey, checkbooks in hand. Of the San Francisco bands, only Steve Miller's and Quicksilver were unaffiliated with any company. According to most accounts, Albert Grossman, manager of Bob Dylan and the Paul Butterfield Blues Band, attempted to bundle Miller, Quicksilver, and the Electric Flag (whose members included Quicksilver's Chicago friend Nick Gravenites) together and offer all three to Columbia's Clive Davis for $100,000. The potential deal fell through and only the Flag—with guitarist Mike Bloomfield, already Grossman's client—signed on, reportedly for $50,000. Steve Miller was wooed successfully by Capitol, and Grossman snagged Big Brother for Columbia after extricating the band from their contract with Chicago's small Mainstream label for $250,000. Dazzled by Quicksilver's set, Cass Elliot of the Mamas and Papas recommended the band to Lou Adler for his new Ode label, and Vanguard (home to Country Joe & the Fish) also expressed interest. However, only Quicksilver walked away from Monterey without a record deal. "We didn't want to sign," said John. "We had no use for [the record labels], and we were unsigned. And we were making more money. We would make double the money of the guys who had a record contract." While the band left the festival without signing on the dotted line, they did not return to San Francisco empty handed, "borrowing" some amplifiers and speakers to enhance the more than sixty dates they had yet to play before 1967 was history.

On the final day of the festival, the band once again spent the morning jamming with the Dead, the Airplane, Hendrix, and the Animals before returning to the arena to hear the nine closing acts, including the Dead, Buffalo Springfield, the Who, and the Jimi Hendrix Experience. (Big Brother, whose Saturday set had not been filmed, delivered a repeat performance in order to get Janis Joplin's electrifying "Ball and Chain" immortalized on celluloid.) Jim Murray, whose days with Quicksilver were numbered, was mesmerized by the opening act, sitar master Ravi Shankar, and would soon acquire the instrument himself.

Two years later, Ralph Gleason wrote that the Monterey Pop Festival, "...proved something which San Francisco rock fans already knew—the San Francisco bands were of a different and more powerful order than the rest of the American rock groups. At Monterey, Big Brother & The Holding Company (with the sensational singer Janis Joplin), the Airplane, Steve Miller, the Grateful

Dead, Country Joe & The Fish, and The Quicksilver Messenger Service stole the show musically from everybody but Jimi Hendrix and the Who. After the Pop Festival, Paul Simon remarked that the San Francisco bands were doing things with music and lyrics that made the rest of U.S. rock music 'sound old-fashioned even before it had begun.'"

Quicksilver and the gear purloined from Monterey, joined the Dead, Big Brother, the Airplane, and Mad River on the Speedway Meadows of Golden Gate Park for the June 21 Summer Solstice Celebration Festival. "It was generally agreed that the spirit of the solstice didn't compare with that of the Be-In," wrote Haight-Ashbury historian Charles Perry. "Maybe it was because of the more confined space of Speedway, or because the crowd was smaller than the Be-In's and *much* smaller than that at the Monterey Pop just three days before. Some people blamed it on the decentralization of the event, which perhaps dissipated the sense of unity." Nonetheless, the celebration went on from sunrise to sunset.

Before the month was out, Quicksilver was filmed in a San Francisco nightclub for inclusion in the low-budget United Artists release *Revolution*. (Precisely when their two studio tracks were recorded has never been noted, nor has Jim Murray's participation in the sessions been verified.) Also appearing in the feature were Steve Miller and Mother Earth, a soulful blues band from Texas fronted by the full-throated Tracy Nelson, who had declined an offer to join Jefferson Airplane before the band replaced Signe Anderson with Grace Slick. Nelson had a less than admirable opinion of the San Francisco bands, telling author Bruce Pollock in 1983, "I thought they were all garbage. The Grateful Dead, Quicksilver, Big Brother—I thought they played their instruments badly and that they had very little understanding of the music. You know, most of the groups considered themselves blues bands. But it was like fourth-generation stuff." (Mother Earth's Martin Fierro would later contribute saxophone and flute to Quicksilver's 1971 album

What About Me.) One can't help but wonder what Nelson felt about Quicksilver's performance when they appeared on the same bill at San Francisco's Straight Theater on July 21. The Straight Theater, larger than both the Fillmore and the Avalon, had formerly been a movie house known as the Haight Theater and was badly in need of renovation. Quicksilver and Big Brother each donated $5,000 toward the project.

A few weeks earlier, Quicksilver was the only prominent San Francisco band to play at another festival held in the Outdoor Theater on Mount Tamalpais on the first day of July, a relatively scaled-back month, as the band had only a dozen gigs, four outside San Francisco—Pasadena, Santa Clara, Lake Tahoe, and San Diego. Of the latter concert, Dick Barnes of the San Diego Union wrote, "The hard-driving blues beat of the Quicksilver Messenger Service is one of the oldest and best-known in San Francisco, the city of sound where new bands are born each day. The QMS has been filling the Fillmore and Avalon ballrooms with its own distinctive brand of music—acid rock mixed with downhome Negro blues—for a year and a half. Gary Duncan, guitar player for the QMS, says, 'We aren't hippies. We know a lot of hippies, and we play for hippies, but really, we're musicians, not hippies.'"

August and September were similarly "quiet", less than twenty dates during the two months, but they did venture out to Santa Barbara and even Denver, Colorado.

After a dozen shows throughout October, including one in San Jose and two in Berkeley, a monumental "Trip or Freak" Halloween bash with the Grateful Dead and Big Brother took place at Winterland, where all three bands had appeared eight days before for a "Marijuana Defense Benefit." The Dead's manager, Rock Scully, recalled in 1996, "The floor at Winterland has plywood over ice and it's *freezing*. It's so cold you can see your breath in there. Still, it's big and brassy and the sound is good…The Dead do up a wonderful orange poster with a multiplied Frankenstein mask on it."

In November, Dino, who had spent the year performing alone at such non-dance clubs as the Kuh Auditorium, began work on a solo album for Columbia's Epic label, although most of the sessions would take place in February and March the following year. Produced by Bob Johnston, the guiding hand of Dylan's *Highway 61 Revisited* and *Blonde On Blonde*, it would not be released until August.

For Quicksilver, November proved to be another relatively slow month, the band playing publically less than a dozen times, but traveling south to Los Angeles to cut several demos at Continental Sound Studios, five of the titles destined to be recorded officially for their first album. They finally accepted a four-year recording contract with Capitol Records, with an advance payment of $40,000, a signing bonus of $10,000, a royalty rate of thirty-three cents per album sold, and additional options amounting to $100,000 for the final two years. Crucially, the band retained publishing rights and insisted on artistic control. "Quicksilver got the best deal of all of us," said the Airplane's Paul Kantner.

Capitol was so eager to have Quicksilver on the label that the company wrote off $50,000 in recording costs after the first attempt at delivering the album, begun in late November and produced by Nick Gravenites and Harvey Brooks of the Electric Flag, as well as Pete Welding, was rejected by the band themselves. "Our thing was to be the loudest band in the world," said Greg. "Knowing how to record a band like that was a huge obstacle to the recording industry." "The first version was never released because it was over-produced and didn't sound like us live," Gary reflected. "We had horns and all the other stuff we could stick on it." Only one bare bones take from the original sessions—"Pride of Man," recorded on December 6—was ultimately used for the completed album. Recording engineer Jay Ranellucci said, "They spent two hundred hours in the studio, threw it all out and started over. The poor engineer doesn't get a break, 'cause there's four of them in the band, with each guy showing up wanting to redo his part. The smoke got pretty thick, too. Some Quicksilver mixing sessions, you didn't dare walk into the room; you'd get a contact high immediately." "The second version—the one that was released—was just us playing like we did live," said Gary, "and then adding a little sweetener here and there to make it sound like a record." John agreed, remarking, "We were pretty lame in the studio, but we were a kick-ass live group." The band spent December 9, 10, and 11 on multiple takes of "The Fool," which would be the album's sole epic (i.e. extended) track, achieving the final version on the 19th.

Quicksilver returned to Lake Tahoe for a second date in early December, then spent the first half of the month laboring on their debut album, which would not be finished by year's end. They managed to fit in a two-night gig at the Avalon Ballroom and two shows at the Shrine Exposition Hall in Los Angeles before the holidays. The summer may have been a bummer as far as the commercialization went, but the communal spirit among the bands was undimmed. They joined members of the Dead, Moby Grape, the Airplane, and the Hell's Angels motorcycle club for a Christmas celebration hosted by Big Brother, complete with a decorated tree, wine, acid, and an abundance of food.

The year concluded with a three-night run at Winterland. Sharing the bill with Quicksilver on the 29th and 30th were Chuck Berry and Big Brother, and on New Year's Eve they were joined by Freedom Highway, Jefferson Airplane, and Big Brother for a blowout that lasted a full twelve hours, from 9 PM to 9 AM, when breakfast was served to the bands and the audience. Eleven of the numbers Quicksilver performed have been released by two different labels, with an additional jam session (including Dino) comprising "Peepin' and Hidin'"/"Ride This Train"/"You Don't Remember Me" available from a third.

All in all, 1967 had been the band's most significant and successful to date, appearing on local television, venturing outside

California several times, being part of not one but two legendary festivals—the Human Be-In and Monterey—and holding out for the most lucrative recording contract offered to any of the San Francisco bands.

*

1968-69

"What *is* certain is that the new music has thoroughly confused the record industry; no one can figure out how to promote it. Since the beginning of this year, the sheer quantity of serious pop, as well as its immense variety, has defied sloganeering. Most of the new musicians are not interested in gimmickry or image making; they just want to make music. It's no longer possible to attract notice with a fancy album cover or way-out name…The best first albums of this year's San Francisco crop come from two of the original underground groups, the Loading Zone and Quicksilver Messenger Service."

Ellen Willis, The New Yorker, July 1968

Few alive then would disagree that 1968 was the most tumultuous year of the Sixties. Martin Luther King and Robert Kennedy were assassinated. The Vietnam War grew worse with the Tet Offensive and the My Lai Massacre. The Democratic convention in Chicago was overshadowed by violent clashes between the police and antiwar demonstrators. The newly-elected Richard Nixon, who would be more despised than President Johnson, made an empty promise to end the war while plotting to do the opposite. Riots caused by a mélange of social ills occurred in Czechoslovakia, Poland, Turkey, Italy, France, Sweden, Brazil, Mexico, and the Soviet Union.

And for the first time, a rock album was the best-selling recording of the year: *Disraeli Gears*, the second by the British power trio Cream, released the previous November. Their two-record *Wheels of Fire* reached #12. Also among the fifty most popular of 1968 were such enduring classics as *Are You Experienced* and *Axis: Bold As Love* by the Jimi Hendrix Experience (who would create their masterpiece, *Electric Ladyland*, before the year was out), Simon & Garfunkel's *Bookends* (as well as their soundtrack to *The Graduate* and two earlier efforts), *Magical Mystery Tour* and *Sgt. Pepper* by the Beatles (who released their self-titled double album at year's end), the self-titled debuts of Steppenwolf and Vanilla Fudge, Dylan's *John Wesley Harding*, Iron Butterfly's *In-A-Gadda-Da-Vida*, *Cheap Thrills* by Big Brother & the Holding Company, the Doors' *Waiting For the Sun* (their only #1 album), and *Time Peace* by the Rascals, one of the best greatest hits compilations of all-time. Soul music increased in widespread acceptance with two by Aretha Franklin (*Lady Soul*, *Aretha Now*), two by the recently deceased Otis Redding (*History of Otis Redding*, *The Dock of the Bay*), *I Wish It Would Rain* (The Temptations), and *Diana Ross & the Supremes Greatest Hits* all placing in the Top 50. Other offerings that have stood the test of time included releases by the Jeff Beck Group, Canned Heat, Judy Collins, Buffalo Springfield, Jethro Tull, the Kinks, Van Morrison, Traffic, Joni Mitchell, and Neil Young. Flying under the radar at the time were two hugely influential albums that signaled a move from elaborate productions and back to basics: *Music From Big Pink* by the Band and *Sweetheart of the Rodeo* by the Byrds. Even the bill of fare on the AM dial showed improvement in 1968, with the Beatles' "Hey Jude" *the* song of 1968, followed by Otis, Simon & Garfunkel, the Rascals, the Doors, the Temptations, the Rolling Stones, Cream, Steppenwolf, and Donovan. On the debit side, listeners also had to tolerate a pair by the 1910 Fruitgum Co. In retrospect, a reasonably convincing case could be made for designating 1968 as the most momentous year for "modern" rock music, at least in the Sixties.

While Big Brother's *Cheap Thrills* was the most successful album from any San Francisco band (since Jefferson Airplane's *Surrealistic Pillow* reached #3 in 1967), making it all the way to #1 and shining a searing spotlight on Janis Joplin (who would soon break off on her own), 1968 saw Jefferson Airplane's *Crown of Creation* hit #6. The Grateful Dead's second effort, *Anthem of the Sun*, an ambitious mixture of live and studio tracks, reached #87. Its single, "Born Cross-

Eyed"/"Dark Star," didn't set any sales records, but the Dead were not about hits. Neither was Quicksilver Messenger Service, whose first album was released in May, first appeared on the Billboard chart on June 22 at #175 and topped out at #63 by October. Their single, "Dino's Song"/"Pride of Man," recorded in March 1968 and December 1967 respectively and also released in May, didn't set the airwaves on fire, nor did a stand-alone release of "Stand By Me" (written by Dino), backed with the novelty tune "Bears" (by a Roger Perkins), recorded in September and issued in November.

On January 17, Quicksilver and the Grateful Dead performed at the Carousel, a 1930s ballroom decorated with fancy chandeliers and drapes that had been the property of the League of Irish Voters. Suitably impressed, both bands entered into a deal with Jefferson Airplane, Big Brother, and the Hell's Angels on February 14 to form Headstone (one source says Triad) Productions and co-own the venue, whose ground floor was occupied by either a carpet showroom or a car dealership. (Recollections differ.) Only Janis Joplin thought it was not a good idea. "It's like turning the Bank of America over to a bunch of six-year-olds! I give you guys six months at best. A bunch of hippies high on acid running a business—my Lord!" Phil Lesh, the Dead's bassist, admitted in his 2005 memoir that the bands "lacked the desire and the business sense to be hands-on daily detail managers. They were too busy making music, playing gigs, etc." With their popularity increasing, Quicksilver began to tour further outside California—including New York, Florida, Arizona, Missouri, Wisconsin, Illinois, Michigan, Ohio—and played the Carousel only two more times in 1968. (In July, legendary concert promoter Bill Graham, who opened New York's Fillmore East in March, took over the Carousel, calling it Fillmore West. The original Fillmore Auditorium had become too small for the burgeoning crowd of San Francisco music enthusiasts.)

A busy January kept the band out of the studio for most of the month, playing for at least ten nights in San Francisco and Eureka, and as far away as Seattle, Washington and Portland, Oregon, five of those dates with the Grateful Dead for an out-of-state jaunt dubbed The Quick & the Dead, which Dead manager Rock Scully remembered as "…the first really full-scale out-of-state Grateful Dead tour. It was the first tour we do that actually has the word *tour* in it. It's also the first traveling Haight-Ashbury hippies-on-the-road show." That brief tour included an additional three dates in February, and on the final night there was trouble. Inspired by the gig's poster, which looked like a Wanted poster out of the Old West, Scully said, "John Cipollina and Bobby Weir take to the outlaw theme a little too realistically.

They both have blank guns and they shoot each other on the street in carefully staged little *High Noon* scenarios. People watching go, 'My God! He just shot him!' And then Cipollina and Freiberg pick Weir up and throw him in the car and drive around to the back of the motel." After the concert, the police, informed of the shoot-out, pulled the equipment truck over and made the road crew unpack everything, including all the sound and recording equipment, to be searched. Nevertheless, the Quick and the Dead tour was a high cultural watermark, Phil Lesh proclaiming it "…a flaming success…the people were coming out in droves, and they were *digging* it. The high point was two nights at the Crystal Ballroom in Portland, a venue that had been built in the twenties for big band dancing. It came complete with a flexible, a spring-loaded, ball-bearing dance floor. What a blast to dance on that floor, as I did to Quicksilver's music on the first night—one couldn't put a foot wrong."

After taking more than week off, Quicksilver spent the remainder of February and early March hitting the Matrix and the Avalon, traveling to Fremont, California, and back to Portland, Oregon, before resuming work on their first album. March 3 was significant for the definitive recording of "Dino's Song." By the time they joined Steppenwolf and Kaleidoscope for a two-night date at the Cheetah in Los Angeles, most of their debut record was "in the can" and was complete before the month was out.

The first day of April found the band playing two live sets on San Francisco's KSAN radio. Of the eleven numbers, four were from the forthcoming album, including two runs through "The Fool" and two of "Who Do You Love," destined for their second project. The rest of the month was filled with more than a dozen gigs. The exact location of their April 4 show is an example of Quicksilver's sometimes cloudy history: An archival two-disc set released in 2008 claims to have been recorded at the Carousel. Two incomplete lists of the band's appearances say it occurred at the Fillmore West. In reality, according to Bill Graham's own records, it was staged at Winterland. On April 14 they played their second—and final—concert at the Carousel, and on the 19th and 20th they managed to appear at the Shrine Exposition Hall *and* the Kaleidoscope in Los Angeles on both nights.

While the band traveled as far as Miami for three dates at the end of May, the most noteworthy event of the month was the release of *Quicksilver Messenger Service*, their first album, its black cover illustrated with the band's striking logo in silver and red by artist Rick Griffin. The strange symbol—also silver—was reminiscent of an Egyptian scarab. Production was credited to Pete Welding and Nick Gravenites and Harvey Brooks of the Electric Flag. The individual back cover portraits of each band member were captured by legendary photographer Jim Marshall.

Clocking in at a hair over a half-hour, there's not one wasted moment on *Quicksilver Messenger Service*, the best debut album by any of the most prominent San Francisco bands. (The Airplane, the Dead, Big Brother, and Country Joe & the Fish all hit their stride with their second offerings.) It opens with "Pride of Man" by folkie Hamilton Camp (who spent the Summer of Love as the opening act for comedian Bill Cosby), a condemnation of nuclear war sung with great gusto by David, Gary joining in on the choruses. Gravenites and Brooks add horns, but they are not as prominent as they would have been on a track by their Electric Flag. For someone who was unschooled on the bass until 1966, David's skill on the instrument is, at the very least, more creative than the simple bass runs Gary had shown him. John's solo features his signature use of the tremolo bar, complete with muted feedback as the cut ends. "Light Your Windows," co-written by Gary and David, has a nice weaving of guitars as well as a jazzy break. Valenti's "Dino's Song," perhaps the most well-known track on the album, has David and Gary sharing the vocal chores and was, unsurprisingly, the A side of its only single. Gary's affinity for jazz is obvious on the six minute-plus instrumental "Gold and Silver" (also known as "Acapulco Gold and Silver," a reference for a particularly potent strain of pot), which he composed with Steve Schuster and is strongly reminiscent of "Take Five," the Dave Brubeck Quartet's 1959 classic written by sax player Paul Desmond. This track swings, with Gary's guitar at the forefront and Greg's drums panning from the left channel to the right. For the entire album, Greg's percussion work is so perfectly suited for each cut that it is easy to overlook. But don't. "Too Long," contributed by manager Ron Polte, is the closest to a conventional pop song the band ever did, so accessible it could have conceivably been a single. John's guitar ping-pongs from left to right at one point, and someone tinkles a piano at the end. The album concludes with the adventurous twelve-minutes known as "The Fool," Gary and David's still-captivating excursion into the realm of psychedelia. The two guitarists mesh so well it's hard to distinguish between them for the first five minutes, at least until Gary's tasteful use of the wah-wah pedal (which can be annoying coming from less talented musicians). David adds a ghostly viola and, seven minutes in, an ethereal vocal. (He later disclosed that the cosmic lyrics, meant to convey the positive spirit of the times, were written under the influence of acid.) This masterpiece, which David has said is the "best of any of the tunes I was involved in" ends with brief, effective feedback and the sudden emergence of an organ. To hear the development of "The Fool," seek out the third volume of *Sweet California Sunshine*, a Japanese import that contains outtakes and rehearsals taped over three days in early December 1967 at Capitol's San Francisco studio.

On May 26, critic Ralph J. Gleason's review of the album was printed by the San Francisco Chronicle along with his reactions to new vinyl by Steve Miller, the Loading Zone, Moby Grape, Blue Cheer, the Great Society, and others: "The Quicksilver album is excellent. It is one of the best of the recent releases and is by far the best example on records of how a San Francisco band actually sounds when you hear it in person. This is the way it is. Capitol did a fine job of recording the band and the Quicksilver, which has had a spotty career in a sense, seems to have come together in all the right ways for a recording and to have stayed that way. I heard them recently and they were exciting and magical. The feeling on the album is beautiful. The Quicksilver play in a way that really projects the joy and the love these bands have at their best. There is a fine jazzy number and a great version of 'Dino's Song' which sounds as if it might be a hit. It turns out to be the kind of album that can be played over and over and over."

Rolling Stone didn't get around to acknowledging the album until its July 6th issue, written by Barry Gifford, who felt producers Gravenites and Brooks exerted too much of an Electric Flag influence. He found their rendition of Camp's "Pride of Man" worthy of praise, complimented John's guitar work, and misidentified Polte's "Too Long" as being by Gravenites. In addition to the Electric Flag, he compared certain aspects of the band to Vanilla Fudge, Country Joe & the Fish, Albert King, Eric Clapton, Procol Harum, and the Yardbirds. "It's inevitable that a group will absorb a certain measure of influence from other bands—and the Quicksilver Messenger Service has emerged on record as a composite of influence, from their overbearing Flag-derived arrangements to a number of easily identifiable characteristics. But, incredibly, their formula works. They have a good, even remarkably honest sound.

Theirs is a much finer record debut than the Grateful Dead's. The only problem seems to be a lack of original direction, something that will be impossible to locate anywhere but in their own individual musical sense." (This is as good a time as any to remember that a review reflects the opinion of only one person, including the author of this book. As Gifford wrote, we all have our own individual musical sense. Amen.)

Is *Quicksilver Messenger Service* dated? It depends, of course, on the age and/or musical tastes of the listener. The reliance on reverb and occasional production "gimmicks" aren't used to mask any possible shortcomings of the band—unlike too often since the late Seventies—but were fresh in 1967-68 and employed to augment the brilliance already present. One may judge the sound of the CD incarnations—even the superior 2015 mixes by Culture Factory—to be overly bright and lacking in depth, but the original masters are, after all, now more than half-a-century old. Magnetic tape does not last forever, especially if it has not been carefully stored.

Quicksilver performed at Bill Graham's Fillmore East in New York for the first time on June 7 and 8. (Also on the bill were the Electric Flag and Steppenwolf.) Their first night was taped, but not available to the general public until Purple Pyramid/Cleopatra Records licensed the recording from Gary's personal archives, highlighted by Dave Thompson's insightful liner notes. In addition to five tracks from their first Capitol album, they ran through "old" favorites "If You Live (Your Time Will Come)," "Smokestack Lightnin'," "Codine," "Mona," "Back Door Man," and "Who Do You Love," as well as Gary's upcoming instrumental workout "Calvary."

Rather than aggressively promote the new album, the band trimmed their concert schedule as well as the lengthy rehearsals they once indulged in. Other than a date in Boston and a return to New York later in the month, they played only four other shows in

June without leaving California. The following month was similarly light on activity, much to Gary's annoyance. He didn't even participate when the band landed a gig in Sunnyvale, California, on July 9. Not wanting to be bothered by drawn-out studio sessions, the band decided to record their second album live.

On Sunday, August 4, Quicksilver was among more than twenty acts (including the Byrds, Steppenwolf, Canned Heat, the Electric Flag, the Dead, Jefferson Airplane) for the First Annual Newport Pop Festival taking place at the Orange County Fairgrounds in Costa Mesa, California. The two-day event drew a crowd in excess of 80,000, far outnumbering Monterey. Except for an August 17 date with the Who in Tempe, Arizona, the band never ventured outside their home state for just eight other shows.

Dino's solo album on Epic, spelled *Dino Valente*, was recorded in Los Angeles, San Francisco, and Nashville. Completed in April, it was not released until August and not available in England until January. Liner notes were contributed by Ralph J. Gleason, who wrote, "Watching him perform—playing and singing—is to watch magic at work in the way he can take the heads of the listeners and meld them all into one with his music…And like magic, elusive in his appearances and in his impact, Dino Valente has finally been captured for nine songs in this album…when you live, breathe and sweat music as he does, everything you do in life is music." Dino himself was quoted as saying, "All I know is that I am evolving. I know where I want to go and what I want to sound like."

What he wanted to sound like was celestial and intimate, yet forceful, favoring spare production, minor chords, all heavily reverberated. The main accompaniment is Dino's twelve-string and flute, augmented by unidentified sidemen providing additional guitar, occasional percussion, and even some tasteful strings. Three tracks exceed seven minutes, including one of the two bonus tracks on the CD version. With the exception of a ghostly studio "experiment" entitled "Test" and Papa John Phillips' "Me and My Uncle," every song was self-composed. Ultimately, the album was a preview of how Quicksilver's sound would be altered when Dino joined them at the end of 1969.

At the end of August, Dino was one of the performers at the three-day Sky River Rock Festival and Lighter Than Air Fair in Sultan, Washington, along with several San Francisco bands—but not Quicksilver. In October, after sharing the bill with Jimi Hendrix and Buddy Miles for three nights at Winterland, he was appearing at the Café au Go Go in New York, where one night Quicksilver manager Ron Polte happened to be in the embarrassingly small audience. Dino complained about how Epic was failing to promote his album. Gary was in town for a two-night stand at the Fillmore East in early November (where "Mona" would be recorded for their next album), and stopped in to hear his friend the following night. When he saw the pathetic turnout, he told Polte, "I'm going to help Dino." Polte felt such a move would affect Quicksilver's momentum, but Gary assured him it wouldn't. Ominously, Gary did not reveal to his manager what he was starting to consider.

On September 17, the band was in the recording studio for the first time since finishing their album to record two non-album tracks that Capitol would release the following month. The A side was Dino's "Stand By Me" (which would eventually be resurrected for the first time on a 1990 CD), and Roger Perkins' curiosity ("Bears") that the band said they did for their children. David handled the lead vocal, John a six-string bass, and Nick Gravenites joined on "background noises" (i.e. grunts and growls). This B side disappeared until Capitol included it on an anthology in 1973.

Judging by the few dates Quicksilver booked during the fall—only eight in September, a dozen in October—one would never guess they had an album to sell, but the band did range as far as Utah, Missouri, Seattle, Wisconsin, Illinois, and Ohio. Their early October show at Shasta College in Redding, California, was sponsored by the student association and KIXE-TV, the school's paper promising that the band "...will send Shasta College swingers into dance orbit with its jazz rock music in the college gymnasium Saturday night. The Ace of Cups, an all-girl band from San Francisco's Avalon Ballroom, will accompany the Quicksilver Messenger Service…The dance will be from 9 p.m. to 1 a.m. Admission will cost $2.50 with a student body card and $3 without a card…Student Richard Riis, assistance social chairman, said the Quicksilver Messenger Service is one of Capitol Records' top recording groups."

On the first of four nights—November 7, 8, 9 and 10—that were broadcast live from the Fillmore West, the band played the version of Bo Diddley's "Who Do You Love" that would comprise the entire first side of their next album, *Happy Trails*. An unedited recording, running nearly half-an-hour, was released on CD in 2014, mistakenly identifying the venue as Winterland. Bill Graham would occasionally schedule concerts at Winterland if ticket demand exceeded the capacity of the Fillmore, but according to Graham's official records, this show was indeed staged at the Fillmore West. And the back cover of *Happy Trails* says, "Live Portions Recorded at Fillmore East and West." (A poster inside the CD states Winterland, so it is possible the location was originally intended to take place there. Such last-minute changes were not unusual.)

With the live side of *Happy Trails* done, Quicksilver entered San Francisco's Golden State Recorders on November 19 for the live-in-the-studio tracks "Maiden of the Cancer Moon" and the thirteen-minute "Calvary," two instrumentals composed by Gary. A third cut was the Roy Rogers classic "Happy Trails," written by his wife, Dale Evans. Lasting less than a minute (because the band could remember only one verse), it featured the sole vocal by drummer Greg Elmore. (In 1970 Janis Joplin recorded a slightly longer version as part of a birthday greeting sent to John Lennon, not issued publicly until 1993.)

After their November broadcast from the Fillmore West in early November, Quicksilver put on less than a dozen shows before 1968 ended. On New Year's Eve, they joined the Grateful Dead, It's A Beautiful Day, and Santana for the annual celebration at Winterland. After the concert, Gary, long frustrated by the band's lack of drive and general ennui, unloaded all of his grievances and told his fellow musicians that he was quitting. "At the end of 1968, I was pretty burned out," he recalled years later. "I didn't want to have anything to do with music at all." Additionally, he had grown tired of his drug usage, admitting, "I did speed every day. Nobody knew I was doing it, they just thought I was crazy. I did so much that I never really came down from it. I don't sleep much; I'm up all the time and it's all right. I figure I've got plenty of time to sleep when I'm dead, you know." David, who correctly regarded Gary as Quicksilver's main source of energy (the band…"just didn't work without him…for me"), was especially stunned, feeling that the band was positioned for a great future. "I was devastated," he added. Capitol was allegedly planning a major promotional push that included sending them on a tour of Europe. According to David, the cowboy waving farewell to his lady on the cover of *Happy Trails* was a tribute to Gary. For many of their fans, Quicksilver Messenger Service's best days were over.

*

"Quicksilver, because they are more concerned with what they do than how much they make, took a year off to re-think their sound-selves. Gary Duncan…left without hard feelings, still a spiritual member and part of them, sort of like leaving home to do whatever on his own for a while. He may or may not join them sometime. In the interim they drew Nicky Hopkins into the family, the fabled Nicky Hopkins who played piano with The Stones and The Beatles…"

Hit Parader, 1969

With U.S. forces in Vietnam increasing to 543,000 it looked as though 1969 stood a better than average chance of being as bleak as the previous year, yet anti-war sentiment was spreading to include older generations. Another bright spot was the banning of the pesticide DDT, indicating a growing concern for the environment, which those "dirty hippies" had been endorsing since at least 1965. Native Americans finally united to protest decades of government mistreatment. In July a human being walked on the moon for the first time. On the negative side, the murders committed by the Charles Manson misfits did nothing to improve the image of young people advocating for alternate lifestyles. And though the positive cultural watershed moment that was the Woodstock Music and Arts Fair resulted in some goodwill from older generations, the chaos of the free Rolling Stones concert at the Altamont Speedway four months later effectively ended the hopeful Age of Aquarius.

Exemplary music continued to be released on a nearly weekly basis: The Rolling Stones' *Let It Bleed*, the Who's fabled *Tommy*, the Band's self-titled second album, Sly & the Family Stone's *Stand!*, three by Creedence Clearwater Revival, debuts by Crosby, Stills & Nash, Joe Cocker, and Santana, and final efforts from Cream and the Beatles (though the postponed *Let It Be* was still to come). From San Francisco's premier bands came the Dead's comparatively laid-back (for them) *Aoxomoxoa*, Janis Joplin's tepid *Kozmic Blues*, Jefferson Airplane's *Volunteers*, and two from Quicksilver Messenger Service.

Without Gary, Quicksilver was a band without direction, spending the early part of the New Year assembling their next recording, *Happy Trails*. "Duncan was gone and we had to come up with an album for Capitol," David recalled in 1997. "We had all this stuff we had recorded live, so we just started listening to it…if we had been out there playing all those big festivals, we could have made a ton of money, and sold a lot of records, but Duncan probably would have died, so it wouldn't have been worth it." The cover art was by George Hunter of the Charlatans, created for Globe Propoganda (Paintings & Portraits), lettering by Kent Hollister, and Logos by Alan Rose.

On the back cover were individual depictions of the band designed after photographs by Fred Roth, Jerry Wainwright, and Jim Smircich. Gary, wearing a cowboy hat, aims a shotgun at the photographer, Greg holds a rifle. John merely poses, David plays a viola, and all wear Western garb. Said John in 1975, "We used to sit on the fence posing with our hats pulled down low, fingers in belts, looking kind of Gary Cooperish. Usually we were too stoned to stand up straight, just living out our cowboy fantasies." Among the more than fifteen people credited on the back cover are Bill Graham, manager Ron Polte and his brother Frank.

The highly revered *Happy Trails* first charted in March and gradually reached #27 by May, outselling their first album and destined to be the one for which they are most remembered, widely acknowledged as the preeminent musical representation of San Francisco in the last half of the 1960s. For the Dead's Jerry Garcia, it was "the most psychedelic album ever recorded." In its review, Rolling Stone hailed it as "...a performance that captures all of the excitement and grandeur of the great days of the scene in a way that is almost too fine to be real." In 2003, the magazine would rank it at #189 on a list of the Top 500 albums of all-time. "I didn't like the album for a long time," Gary admitted several years later, "could not even listen to it at all. But now when I hear it, I can see why people like it. I think a lot of people like that record because it reminds them of a time in their lives when life was easier and more fun...back when they were young."

Clocking in at fifty minutes-plus—ten more than recommended for highest fidelity in the days of vinyl—*Happy Trails* required only a volume tweak for maximum enjoyment. Parts One and Two of Bo Diddley's (Elias McDaniel) "Who Do You Love" bookends the "suite" of Who/When/Where/How/Which/Who Do You Love that takes up the entire first side of the album, credited in order to Diddley, Gary, Band & Fillmore Audience, John, David, and Diddley. "Where" is idly, subtle jamming and sound effects that form a "call" from the band and a "response" of shouting and clapping from the crowd. The second side kicks off with a live run through Diddley's "Mona," followed by two studio tracks composed by Gary, "Maiden of the Cancer Moon" and the majestic "Calvary," the peak of Quicksilver's non-concert recordings. "We were really swacked when we recorded that one," said John. Listeners can catch their breath during Greg's brief reading of "Happy Trails." In June, Capitol released a single of "Who Do You Love"/"Which Do You Love," which charted the following month and rose to #91, a not much better showing than their last ("Stand By Me"/"Bears" #110).

Comparisons between Capitol's *Happy Trails* and Sonic Boom's mislabeled *Winterland November 1968* (2014) are illuminating. The running time of "Who Do You Love" on the official album is 25:22, the edited performance of "Mona" is 6:53, described as edited because on the posthumous release, "Mona" lasts for 18:25 and includes the When/Where/How/Which section that Capitol grafted onto "Who Do You Love" as well as generous quotes from "Maiden of the Cancer Moon" and "Calvary," which the band would record in the studio twelve days later. As for "Who Do You Love" on the Sonic Boom disc, it runs 27:07 and is noticeably different from Capitol's version. In essence, the Sonic Boom recordings are as they were performed; Capitol and/or the band obviously did some editing.

Quite likely after seeing how reasonably well *Happy Trails* fared in the marketplace, Jefferson Airplane and the Grateful Dead issued live albums in 1969, both—*Bless Its Pointed Little Head* and *Live Dead*—now rightly regarded as classics.

Quicksilver did not perform live until April 24, when they went to Chicago to participate in the Cosmic Joy-Scout Jamboree. John, David, and Greg were joined by their friend Nick Gravenites, who was then living with manager Ron Polte, on vocals. (Six songs by Muddy Waters, Michael Bloomfield, Paul Butterfield and others were included on Waters' *Fathers and Sons* four months later, the album partly produced by Pete Welding, who had worked on Quicksilver's debut.) The trio played only a handful of gigs during June and July, joined by their sound engineer Dan Healy on one occasion, Gravenites for two others, dubbing themselves as either Nicksilver or the Quick and the Nick. They also may or may *not* have contributed to three tracks of Gravenites' Columbia solo album *My Labors*. The inner sleeve credits stated that they were recorded by "Nick and anonymous friends," rumored for years to be John, David, and Greg, most likely unnamed due to Gravenites and Quicksilver being on different labels.

In July they entered Wally Heider Studios in San Francisco to begin their third album, which would include their rendition of Gravenites' "Holy Moly" (which the composer had done live with Michael Bloomfield on *My Labors*) and the Cipollina/Gravenites track "Joseph's Coat," Nicky Hopkins' first recording with the band. "Quicksilver was the first band I'd played in without a piano," said John. "I always missed the keyboard, so when Gary left, instead of trying to replace a guitarist, I looked for a piano player. Nicky was the best. It seemed natural to me. Besides, we became good friends right from the start." "They just hit it off," David recalled. "That's probably why he joined Quicksilver, 'cause they hit it off so well." Nicky's masterwork, "Edward, (The Mad Shirt Grinder)," was done on the 14th, John's "Three Or Four Feet From Home" on the 23rd. Work on the album—to be called *Shady Grove*—prevented them from playing many dates during August, Nicky not joining them onstage until a Fillmore West engagement on the 22nd and at the Family Dog On the Great Highway the following night.

Nicky traveled to Bethel, New York, to play piano for Jefferson Airplane at the Woodstock festival in the early morning hours of August 16. Two weeks later, he was back with Quicksilver for the Second Annual Sky River Rock Festival near Seattle, Washington, which included other San Francisco acts Country Joe & the Fish and the Steve Miller Band.

The slow progress of cutting the third album, which required the talents of four engineers and was produced by John Palladino, resumed in September. The band moved from Wally Heider Studios to Pacific High Recorders, where Gary's "Maiden of the Cancer Moon" and "Calvary" had been recorded the previous November. For the past nine months, Gary and Dino had been traversing the highways of America on Triumph Bonneville motorcycles. In New York they shared a rundown apartment, and then attempted to put together a band called the Outlaws, which came to nothing despite expanding their search for musicians to Nashville, Muscle Shoals, and Hollywood. They junked their original bikes, opted for Harley Sporters, and made one final run from Los Angeles to Oregon before returning to San Francisco.

In mid-October, the band began mixing the album. One night they decided to take a break and catch Joe Cocker and the Grease Band, who were playing four dates at the Fillmore West. Also at the show were none other than Gary and Dino. After the concert, all six musicians returned to the studio to listen to a playback of Quicksilver's next release. The nine tracks featured more vocals and keyboards than their first two efforts, as well as less fiery guitar, culminating in a subdued and even bucolic sound. Indeed, the title song, "Shady Grove," was a traditional folk number that has been recorded with varying lyrics by several different artists, including the Dead's Jerry Garcia and friend David Grissman on an album of the same name in 1996. (Quicksilver credited the composer as being a P.O. Wands.) According to premier San Francisco historian Joel Selvin, Gary and Dino were less than impressed, to put it mildly: "...they were openly arrogant and insulting" and "bluntly described the album as a piece of shit and announced they could easily make one better." The spirit of musical camaraderie prevailed, however, and the seeds of a "new" Quicksilver were sown. Rehearsals were so satisfying that David told Ron Polte that the vocal blend could make them the next Crosby, Stills and Nash. "For a while it was a hell of a band," said David. (In 2009, a dozen practice tracks with Gary and Dino—recorded in a Corte Madera studio during late 1969 and early 1970—were released. Among the selections was Dino and Gary's "Subway," later a staple of the band's live performances.

Capitol released *Shady Grove* before the year was out, and after it first charted on January 24, 1970, it began climbing to #25, slightly outselling *Happy Trails*. If listeners were anticipating another flaming series of tunes, they were surprised, disappointed, or both. The reviews, for the most part, were positive. An unnamed critic for *Playboy* wrote: "I think *Shady Grove* is an ecology record, verdant and growing, happy as a summer Back Then when you could idle your own motor and dig on the harvest or the green fields...A very beautiful record, extremely nice piano by Nicky Hopkins who seems to have melded into the group without a seam and they're damn sharp about it." *Stereo Review*: "The band's sound is a cross between the Stones and Neil Young with a lot of Byrds thrown in for good measure. That's pretty heavy company to be in, but Quicksilver holds its own and the album can be listened to frequently without growing tiresome." The reaction of *Rolling Stone*'s Gary Von Tersch was decidedly mixed, confessing he missed "the old Quicksilver" but considered the sound of the new album to be "...more precise, more lyrical, more textured." He concluded by saying, "Fine music is still the result—but that rock and roll, free-form jamming quality seems to have been sacrificed."

One of the most glowing reviews was published in the January 23, 1970 edition of the *San Diego Union*, critic Carol Olten calling the album "...a woodsy collection of vignettes etched in suede and buckskin...old-timey country and western with space age additions...among the best produced by a rock group turned country since the Byrds came along with *Sweetheart of the Rodeo*...full of freak noises, folksiness and mysticism...an album of remarkable contrasts." An unidentified critic concurred, saying *Shady Grove* was their best album thus far, and that the band "...looks at the peaceful country with the occasional help of extrusive rock and roll…and makes its own special music and searches for peace of mind. The four try to speak the truth as they see it, and nothing but the truth. Quicksilver's music is sweet and haunting beyond words. And the wall-to-wall hard music is naturally loud and makes you forget the semi-virtuosos like Iron Butterfly or Led Zeppelin. And as the sun colors the flowers, their music colors their life."

The predominantly green gatefold cover, once again designed by Globe Propaganda, depicted a lone young woman (the abandoned maiden from the *Happy Trails* illustration?) seated beneath a tree in—yes—a shady grove, a surrey parked nearby, her only company a brown horse, a blue squirrel, and a frog perched on a mushroom. Inside were individual black-and-white photos of the band members and a large group shot captured in an Old West saloon, John and Greg (wearing cowboy hats) playing poker, David with his viola, and a smiling Nicky seated at a piano.

The underrated *Shady Grove*, one of 1969's forgotten or undiscovered gems, gives David Freiberg in particular an opportunity to shine, writing or co-writing three of its nine selections, displaying more of his expertise on viola than he had previously (or ever would again), and handling the bulk of the vocals. The title track blasts out of the speakers with a classically-tinged piano and a muscular Bo Diddley beat, sounding little like Quicksilver did at the beginning of the year and quite dissimilar to other versions of "Shady Grove." As it fades, someone imitates the croaking of a frog. We have definitely followed the band to the countryside of life. "Flute Song," featuring David's breathy, tender vocal and understated viola, wafts along at a leisurely pace, thanks to Greg's subtle percussion and delicate piano and guitar. "3 or 4 Feet From Home," the album' shortest cut, is John's first solo composition and vocal, the dog bark that opens the song contributed by Nicky. David's passionate vocal on his "Too Far"—which ends with a rousing bossa nova shuffle—is ample proof that he could easily have combined his folk roots and rock sensibilities a made a solid album on his own had Quicksilver fallen apart after Gary's departure. His double-tracked vocal on the band's propulsive rendition of Nick Gravenites' "Holy Moly" is similarly impressive. "Joseph's Coat," written by John and Gravenites, sounds almost like a sequel to Gary's "Calvary" due to its dramatic, heavily echoed chorale and ethereal, prolonged fade-out. The album's second longest track, the contemplative "Flashing Lonesome" by David and Gravenites, benefits from sensitive interplay between John and Nicky, ending with an unexpected free-form jam. If the album has a clear candidate for a single it's "Words Can't Say," which Capitol released as the B-side of "Holy Moly" the month before the album was available. Had it been given the A-side the disc may have fared better instead of not even charting in the Top 100. Done in ¾ time and punctuated by John's tremolo touches and David's soaring viola, it's something of a country ballad and serves as a perfect lead-in to *Shady Grove*'s undeniable highlight, Nicky's "Edward, (The Mad Shirt Grinder)," a keyboard tour de force complimented by Greg's driving drums that includes a slow, bluesy segment accompanied by John's multi-tracked guitar. Calling the piece dazzling does not do it justice. Incredibly, Nicky came up with the piece after an immediate flash of inspiration, as David recalled: "I was overdubbing a bass track and all of a sudden Nicky put his hand to his head and got this huge smile on his face. He ran and got a bunch of music paper and started scribbling like crazy. I don't know whether my bass overdub inspired him, but he wrote out the whole thing and it was just a joy. We always kept a two-track going, just for all the little 'doodads' he played in between." (Volume One of the *Sweet California Sunshine* trilogy, a 2023 Japanese import, includes four interesting outtakes from the *Shady Grove* sessions: "Edward," "Joseph's Coat," "Holy Moly," and "Shady Grove.")

December 6 was the date of the infamous free Rolling Stones concert at the Altamont Speedway in Livermore, California. San Francisco was represented by Jefferson Airplane and Santana, the

Grateful Dead declining to play after hearing that the Hell's Angels had assailed Airplane singer Mary Balin when he tried to stop them from beating members of the audience. Quicksilver dodged a bullet by loaning the promoters some of the equipment they had acquired at the Monterey Pop Festival and remaining safe at home.

The band, which had not performed live since late August, played a warm-up show without Gary or Dino in Brown's Valley, California, on December 22. On New Year's Eve, Bill Graham mounted celebratory concerts at both the Fillmore West (Santana, It's A Beautiful Day, Elvin Bishop Group, Joy of Cooking) and Winterland (Jefferson Airplane, Quicksilver Messenger Service, Sons of Champlin, Hot Tuna) from nine o'clock at night to nine in the morning, with breakfast served at each venue, as had been done in 1967. Graham, however, was at his Fillmore East in New York, where a portion of Jimi Hendrix's sets were released the next year as his *Band of Gypsys* album. Quicksilver had appeared there twice in 1968, but not since.

The December 31 set with Gary and Dino back in the fold included the duo's "Subway," Dino's "Mojo" (not recorded in the studio until 1972), Dino's "City of Stone" (there never would be a studio version), "I Believe" by an unknown writer (though the moody lament certainly sounds like a Valenti composition), and "Mona" (nearly two minutes longer than the *Happy Trails* version). Promoting the new album were "Words Can't Say" by David and D. Jewkes, and Nicky's showcase, "Edward, (The Mad Shirt Grinder)," a bit faster than the studio incarnation and with John's guitar more prominent. It's worth noting that "Subway," "City of Stone," and "I Believe" all seem to be reflective of Gary and Dino's unhappy time in New York. These seven tracks were issued on CD in 2016 as *More Happy Trails 1969*, an important document of reasonably acceptable sound quality, and a preview of what Quicksilver would become during the following decade.

*

PHOTO SECTION

David, Gary, Greg, John, Jim (1966)

Montery, 1967

John, Jim (Montery, 1967)

With Harvey Brooks

Debut Album (Artist: Rick Griffin)

Happy Trails (Artist: George Hunter)

John, Gary, Nicky, David--1969

Shady Grove (Globe Propaganda)

Dino Valenti

David, Gary, Dino—1970

Just For Love (Artists: George Osaki/Mike Cantrell)

What About Me (Artist: Mike Cantrell)

Quicksilver, 1971 (Artist: Burray Olson)

Comin' Thru (Artist: Burray Olson)

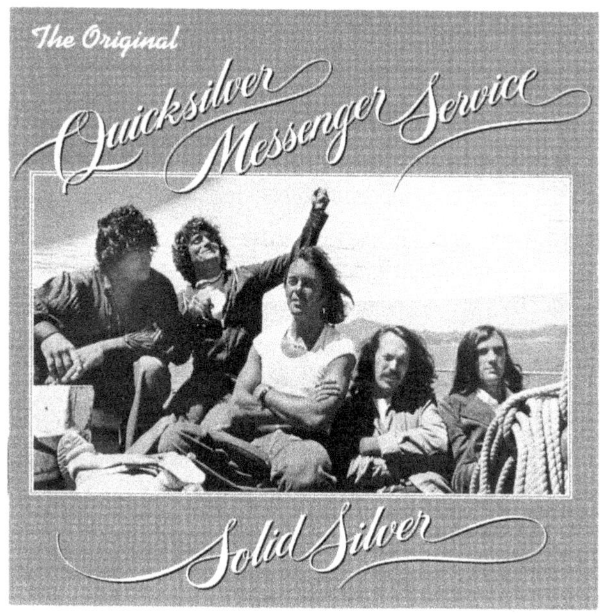

Solid Silver

1970-1971

"With any luck at all, The Quicksilver Messenger Service is going to be one of the biggest musical and box office successes San Francisco has seen. I'm glad they're back."

Ralph J. Gleason, San Francisco Chronicle, February 9, 1970

The calendar may have indicated that a new decade had dawned, but the Seventies would prove to be an extension of the Sixties for at least the next five years. The war in Vietnam spread to Cambodia. Four antiwar demonstrators at Kent State University in Ohio were murdered by the National Guard, moving Neil Young to write "Ohio" and immediately record it with Crosby, Stills and Nash. The Environmental Protection Agency was created to combat pollution, resulting in the first Earth Day. On January 4, the Beatles—minus John Lennon—recorded for the final time; in April Paul McCartney issued his official declaration that the group was no more. Other dark news in the world of music: Jimi Hendrix died on September 18, followed by the death of Janis Joplin on October 4.

Psychedelic music was passé before the new decade dawned, gradually replaced by gentler, more introspective music as the age of the singer/songwriter began. Making the largest impacts in 1970 were James Taylor's *Sweet Baby James*, Cat Stevens' *Tea For the Tillerman*, Joni Mitchell's *Ladies of the Canyon*, Van Morrison's *Moondance*, Neil Young's *After the Goldrush*, and *Déjà vu* from Crosby, Stills, Nash & Young. Bob Dylan's *New Morning* was his first "important" album since 1966, Stephen Stills' released his first solo outing, and even Led Zeppelin's third contained more acoustic music than listeners expected. Eleven rock albums reached #1, including the Beatles' *Let It Be*, Simon & Garfunkel's *Bridge Over Troubled Water*, and the first *Woodstock* soundtrack. The Rolling

Stones were MIA with new music, but offered *Get Yer Ya-Yas Out*, a souvenir of their 1969 tour and one of the greatest live albums of all-time.

Jefferson Airplane, in the process of splintering, only managed to release a single ("Mexico"/"Have You Seen the Saucers?") and a greatest hits collection (humorously titled *Worst*), but Jorma Kaukonen and Jack Casady's Hot Tuna offered a wholly satisfying surprise with their live self-titled acoustic debut. Other Bay Area artists were flourishing: Creedence Clearwater Revival's *Cosmo's Factory* was to become their most popular album, Santana's *Abraxas* (featuring a reworking of "Black Magic Woman" by Fleetwood Mac's Peter Green) was a monster, and the Grateful Dead seemed to follow the example set by Quicksilver's folk-influenced *Shady Grove* and created two largely blues and countrified classics, *Workingman's Dead* and *American Beauty*, considerably expanding their audience.

Quicksilver Messenger Service also recorded and released two albums in less than six months, thanks chiefly to the growing dominance of the prolific Dino Valenti, composer of their two most well-known songs. His influence over the band's sound and direction effectively split their fans into two camps: those who preferred the "old" Quicksilver of *Happy Trails*, and those who didn't care as long as the music continued. The conventional line among some that Dino "ruined" Quicksilver is ludicrous. Dino *changed* Quicksilver, his influence, drive, and frequently soul-stirring songs injecting new life into the band. And a band changes or it dies, commercially, creatively, or both. As Roger Daltrey of the Who sang in 1978, music *must* change. The Beatles did not keep turning out material like "I Want To Hold Your Hand" from 1964 to 1969, and neither could Quicksilver churn out variations on "The Fool" forever. They had started to explore new musical avenues before Dino joined and were not the same in 1969 as they had been in 1967. The band circa 1970 was neither better nor worse than 1968—they were different. And consider this: What if Dino had been a member of the band as far back as 1965, as originally planned? Obviously, we will never know, but it's something to think about...

Today there is more music available from 1970 than any other year of Quicksilver's existence, two studio albums and no less than eight live dates or rehearsal sessions released posthumously. The year was also the band's most active on the concert circuit since 1968, playing well over 40 times and ranging wider than ever, including New York, Texas, Massachusetts, Colorado, Ohio, Kansas, Florida, Hawaii, and of course, California.

In January, they traveled to New York for their first gig of the year (and the only one of the month), a two-night stand at Bill Graham's Fillmore East. It was just their third time at the theater and had not been there since November 1968. Back in San Francisco, they played two nights at the Family Dog At the Great Highway in early February, prompting Ralph J. Gleason to post an enthusiastic review ("The Quicksilver's Strong Comeback") in the San Francisco Chronicle: "What has happened is that all the elements have finally gelled. The QMS (with Greg Elmore, one of the steadiest drummers in rock) swings like mad and Johnny Cipollina's lead guitar is lyrical and inventive and David Freiberg's vocals are excellent. Now with Gary Duncan sharing lead guitar chores with Cipollina and singing (he did 'Mona' at the Family Dog and I hope they record it all over again) a new dimension is added. Another dimension is the presence of Hopkins who is an amazing and original pianist...Hopkins gives the whole sound a different timbre. Then there is Dino Valente (sic). He is one of the truly great performers and composers of the whole San Francisco musical renaissance and he has been about to burst out as a popular star for some time. This will do it. Dino has found a home. With Duncan and Freiberg, he makes up a heavy front vocal line for the Messengers and he is writing and singing superbly. Everything seems to work with the Messengers now...It is really a very impressive band. The musical variety is considerable...The ensemble sound is as heavy and complex as any I have heard in rock."

Prior to the gig Gleason caught, the band laid down a dozen rehearsal/demo tracks at a studio in Corte Madera, California in late 1969 and early 1970, eventually issued on a Charly CD titled *Castles In The Sand* by the Artistry Music Limited/Snapper Music label in 2009. What's immediately notable is the autocratic attitude Dino was known for as the disc opens with him claiming he'll be "dead" if Quicksilver remains the same as it was before he joined. During "Subway" he tells John when to take a solo, complains to the engineer that the sound is too loud, and tells Nicky to play softer. David occasionally sings, but for the most part it is Dino's show. There are surprising readings of Hank Williams' "May You Never Be Alone" from 1950 and country songwriter Cindy Walker's "Warm Red Wine" from 1949. Such standards as "I Know You Rider" and "Look Over Yonder Wall" are given liberal interpretations, but "The Fool" is not the Duncan/Freiberg epic from the first Quicksilver album. Rather it is another rambling composition from Dino in which he worries about being thought a fool or "crazy." The latter is a word destined to crop up more than once in his future writing.

The first taped example of 1970 Quicksilver in concert occurred on March 29 at the Old Mill Tavern in—where else?—Mill Valley, where only one ("Mona") of the eight tracks made available on Purple Pyramid/Cleopatra Records 2013 release of the performance dated back to earlier times.

Following Michael Bloomfield, Nick Gravenites & Friends, Quicksilver tore through "Subway," "The Truth," "Mona," "Baby Baby," "Rain" (never recorded in the studio), and "Mojo." According to *Rolling Stone*'s coverage of the show one month later, "The crowd got on its feet and shaking during the last half of the Silver set, when Valente (sic) called out James Cotton, who blew his harp for awhile and then joined Dino in a trading-four-bars duet on 'Bye-Bye Baby.' Big James would yell, 'I say, bye-BYE baby!' and Dino would pick up on his riff and implore, with a burlesque tone, 'Oh, PLEASE don't say bye-bye.' At one point they stood—almost head-to-head—in mock angry stances wailing a tight counterpoint, each unable to outdo the other, the tension growing, the crowd really excited, until they backed off each other's actions in a smooth transition. It was a real springtime welcome, with the crowd passing dope, Red Mountain and Frisbees about with easy abandon." Happily, Cotton's contributions to Quicksilver's set appear as "Blues Jam #1" and "Blues Jam #2" on the CD.

The disc's liner notes by Dave Thompson quote a British reporter as writing, "Valenti dressed and acted like an inspired jester. He bopped all over the stage, making the band work to, and through, him. His big, clear voice gave every number a unity…I can still hear the cheers." David Freiberg felt the same, opining that Dino "figured that's what we needed, and…that's how he already was. That's how it had to be. If he was there, he had to be out front. And none of us…I wasn't that way, and Duncan wasn't that way…so maybe it's what we needed." He was to later change his tune about Dino's overbearing command of the spotlight, but admitted that there was still "a lot of good stuff happening."

Quicksilver was back in New York in early April for another two shows at the Fillmore East on the 3rd and 4th. The next night their performance at New York's Stony Brook College—where they had played exactly one month before—was recorded but remained unheard until 2015. The two-disc Purple Pyramid/Cleopatra release, again admirably supplemented by a Dave Thompson essay, is a mixture of older ("Mona," "Pride of Man") and as-yet-unrecorded numbers such as "The Truth" and "Long Haired Lady." David was able to be the center of attention, albeit briefly, for *Shady Grove*'s "Too Far."

After five more dates in April, the band took a month-long break to prepare for a Major Move, disclosed by *Rolling Stone*'s May 28 issue: "Quicksilver Messenger Service are in Oahu, Hawaii, sequestered in a big country house they've rented for living and recording purposes. They have a 16-track machine from Capitol and will stay there until June 4th, when they do a week of concerts in Honolulu."

The Hawaiian sojourn was Dino's idea, supported by Gary. David didn't think it was a good one, but was outvoted by the rest of the band. "I thought it was a really silly idea,"he said. "There are no studios there, but they said, 'We're going to build our own studio!'" Relations between the authoritarian Dino and David, who had more or less been in a position of leadership during the recording of *Shady Grove*, were not particularly harmonious. Not helping matters was Dino's insistence that David quit the Grateful Dead's softball team. "When Dino and Gary came back, a lot of stuff changed politically in the band," said recording engineer Dan Healy. "It was one of those 'too hot to handle' situations that eventually got top-heavy and toppled over." Manager Ron Polte, who would resign as their manager before the year was over, agreed: "...when Dino moved in...it was hard to oppose anything and the stuff we worked on was mostly his. A democracy turned into a dictatorship." Apparently no one was willing to argue with the author of "Get Together" and who, to be fair, was the most ambitious songwriter in the band, currently using the composing alias Jesse Oris Farrow.

The band's Hawaiian destination was the Opaelua Lodge, a redwood building owned by a family whose daughter was a Quicksilver fan. Located on an isolated former sugarcane plantation accessible only by seven miles of dirt road, its mountaintop vista offered a clear view of Pearl Harbor. A generator was required because the lodge had no electricity, just gaslights, and it ran constantly. "What a waste of money!" Gary later admitted. Healy set the studio up in the living room, and a multi-level subterranean military bunker left over from World War II was used for echo effects "...with speakers and a microphone," Gary said. "At night you could turn the microphone up and you'd hear all these critters running around and if you walked outside the house at night you could hear the music coming up out of the ground—it was magical!"

Like David, Nicky went to Hawaii reluctantly. "Dino had a real gift of gab and would be able to talk any one of us around his little finger," he said. "We were all living on top of each other and the personality clashes were just so bad." He moved into the master bedroom and kept the shades pulled down and, disgusted by insects, sealed cracks around the window frames with electrical gaffer's tape. When he wasn't needed in the studio he stayed in his room drinking tea and eating from a large stash of candy bars. Dino seemed to be envious or resentful of anyone else's talent, especially Nicky's. Healy remembered that Dino "would walk in the studio and just start flipping on somebody, which is not conducive to creativity, and Nicky was very sensitive to that stuff; he could sniff a vibe right out of the air. Because of his accomplishments, he was not prone to want to put up with it and I can't say that I blame him. Nicky Hopkins did not need to take crap from anybody about anything." The keyboard virtuoso grew so agitated that he returned to the mainland before the rest of the band.

In 2014 the British label Gonzo Multimedia issued the *Hawaii 1970* CD, a live album of Quicksilver's performance at the Honolulu Convention Center on June 13. Limited to the first edition was a bonus disc of a band rehearsal at the Opaelua Lodge on June 4. The twelve-page booklet included eight color photographs contributed by Gary, taken at the Convention Center as well as Honolulu's Diamond Head Crater Festival on June 7. The majority of the music on both discs consisted of material that would be released on their next two albums. Between recording sessions they played an Oahu nightspot called the Red Vest Inn on June 12 and 13, joined by the Grateful Dead and the New Riders of the Purple Sage, a portion of their performance the second night released in 2016 by Purple Pyramid/Cleopatra Records in the *Live Across America 1967-1977* box set. The compilation also includes the June 4 rehearsal session, which is sufficiently interesting to warrant at least one listening. Three takes of John's instrumental "Cobra" (erroneously credited to Farrow/Valente [sic]) run fifteen minutes, and over nine takes of David's "Won't Kill Me" go on for more than twenty-six, with no vocal until nineteen minutes in. Dino's "Good Old Rock and Roll" consists of several run-throughs lasting ten minutes. There are two acoustic takes of John's "Cobra" (this time credited to him) and one of Dino's "Just For Love," accompanied by acoustic guitar and piano and marginally superior to the official studio recording. While Dino's high-pitched, nasally vocals may be an acquired taste, the same can be said of Bob Dylan, Neil Young, and Rush's Geddy Lee. As for the rest, two brief tracks—"Guitar Jam" and "Drums"—are listed as Quicksilver Messenger Service contributions and are of no consequence.

By June 18 Quicksilver was back in San Francisco for five nights at the Fillmore West. Despite David's recollection of the Hawaiian sessions being "disastrous…nothing was finished," the band had recorded enough material for nearly two albums. The basic tracks were judged acceptable when first evaluated, but not after Dino had taken the tapes to Capitol and took over post-production. "He screwed up the sounds," said Nicky. "He took a lot of the bottom end out and added far too much echo on the instruments as well as on his voice and the mix was shitty as well. It was a real shame because they sounded great untouched."

The album, *Just For Love*, first entered the sales chart on August 22 and peaked at #27, the same position *Happy Trails* had achieved, and two notches below *Shady Grove*. Its only single, "Fresh Air"/"-Freeway Flyer," charted in October and rose to #49, Quicksilver's most successful attempt at a radio hit. *Just For Love*, its fractious creation and disappointing audio quality aside, is a consistently strong album, widely acknowledged as the band's most underrated. It is somewhat thematic and unified (though *Rolling Stone* disagreed), opening with an airy instrumental called "Wolf Run (Part 1)"—inspired by John's pet wolf?—and the title song, both of which are reprised at the album's conclusion. In between are four tracks written by Dino and one by John.

Predictably, *Rolling Stone*'s review attacked the album's production: "Unlike the other two Quicksilver studio albums, which were carefully recorded and mixed, this one sounds like it was thrown together with little or no preparation beforehand. Most of the vocals are terribly recorded...The only two songs that are really up to par come back-to-back on side two. 'Gone Again' is the loveliest thing Quicksilver has ever recorded. The guitars of Cipollina and Duncan blend softly with Hopkins' piano that creates a beautiful mood that fits perfectly with newcomer Dino Valenti's voice. 'Fresh Air' has a lot of singing in it but almost no lyrical content, but no matter. It moves, has good solos by Duncan and Hopkins and is the only song on the album that sounds at all like the old Quicksilver... Quicksilver has three proven songwriters in Duncan, Freiberg and Valenti...and if they take enough time and care in the studio, they should be able to produce some more fine music." The prickly but always entertaining Robert Christgau of The Village Voice, no great admirer of the band, gave the album a B- rating and felt its "echoed vocals and imprecise impressionistic accompaniment" were more representative of San Francisco's "ballroom ambience" than the live cuts on *Happy Trails*. He also dubbed "Fresh Air" the "quintessential Quicksilver anthem" and complimented John and Gary's guitar work.

The colorful gatefold cover of *Just For Love*, primarily the work of artists George Osaki and Mike Cantrell, depicted David, John, and Gary wielding otherworldly guitars, Greg at his drums and Nicky playing a massive variation of a pipe organ. The heads of Dino and some sort of mystical maiden, a star twinkling at her fingertips, floated in a cloud hovering over a mountain, a heavy construction vehicle inexplicably parked nearby. The eleven color photographs inside were credited to Laura Lambe and Woody Woodridge. A supporting "cast" of twenty three individuals—including Dan Healy, Ron Polte, Frank Polte, and executive producer John Palladino—were listed, and a "Ladies Section" amounted to an additional twenty-six names. As for the band members, Dino was described as the "World's most magical brat" (Alias—The Hammer), Gary the "World's most funky Saint," David the "World's most cuddly Devil," John the "World's most benign carnivore," Nicky the "World's most polite monster," and Greg—identified as Gregory—the "World's most rhythmic mystic." The extensive arsenal of musical instruments is cited (electric guitar, slide guitar, acoustic guitar, bass, piano, congas, flute, maracas, woodblock—but no mention of David's viola) and so are the types of firearms favored by Dino (P.38, 9m.m.), Gary (.44 Magnum) and Greg (.44 Magnum), evidently employed to let off steam between sessions. Dino, the Magical Brat, is also credited with the use of "Ginseng & various assorted psychic and visual effects."

Just For Love, running a little over thirty-nine minutes, contains nine of the nineteen tracks Quicksilver would release before the end of the year. The remastered edition released by Culture Factory in 2015 is an improvement over the original CD and Capitol's 1970 vinyl. While there is still a surplus of reverb (Dino's vocals may just as well have been recorded in an empty warehouse), the bass, drums and piano are mixed more prominently, much to the benefit of the overall sound. "Wolf Run (Part 1)" opens with leisurely played flute and congas, followed by an equally casual first installment of the title song and John's aggressive "Cobra," a nearly five-minute instrumental reminiscent of the "old" Quicksilver. Dino's inordinately long (ten-plus minutes) "The Hat" begins informally with the band getting ready before it settles into a rambling groove. It could actually have been a rehearsal; at least Nicky's piano is no longer buried in the mix. (Quicksilver fans who heard "Big Dumb Man" on Carly Simon's 2000 album *The Bedroom Tapes* had to be surprised when a familiar thirty-year-old tune came from their speakers: A quick check of the credits revealed that the track "Contains samples of 'The Hat' performed by The Quicksilver Messenger Service Band, courtesy of Capitol Records.") After a false start, Dino's "Freeway Flyer"chugs along with some of John's best playing and driven by Nicky's percussive piano. For a change, echo elevates the effect of

Dino's subdued vocal and is appropriate for the hypnotic, tender "Gone Again," arguably the most moving piece this edition of the band ever recorded. John and Gary's guitars mingle perfectly with piano, bass, and softly played congas. (Dino's use of the then-popular term "groovy" dates the song; the word would eventually become as clichéd and annoying as today's too-frequent reliance on "awesome" and "incredible.") "Gone Again" is the perfect lead-in to the instantly appealing "Fresh Air," the band's biggest commercial success. Extolling the virtues of the once illegal noble weed, the song has a memorable chorus, great solos by Gary and Nicky, and was one of the bright spots of AM radio in 1970. The reprise of the title song is sung more forcefully than the first and adds David's uncredited viola to heighten the drama; the flute and congas on Part 2 of "Wolf Run" that concludes the album are taken at a faster clip.

In July, Nicky decided not to return to England and purchased a house in Mill Valley. Though the August 6 issue of *Rolling Stone* reported that he was "no longer tinkling the ivories for Quicksilver Messenger Service," he hadn't completely severed ties with the band. In November he joined David and Greg in the studio to complete his sole contribution to the second album they had started in Hawaii. Stone also said Capitol had scheduled the next album for release in September, which turned out to not be true.

One significant advantage of having been a member of Quicksilver was Nicky's acquisition of a Countryman Pickup controller, designed specifically for him by Carl Countryman for live dates. Originally the piano had to be amplified by running a contact microphone through the soundboard, but the new invention allowed Nicky to "...get both the volume *and* the tone through the sound system so well," he later enthused. Gary remembered that Countryman had been working on the device since the end of

1969 and that the pickup went "...into the piano and clips on to the harp and it's got pick-ups that fit across the strings to take a grand piano and make it electric." Engineer Dan Healy helped

Countryman develop the equipment, saying, "…Nicky was the first pianist in rock 'n' roll whose sound was out there."

Without Nicky, the band spent the remainder of summer playing shows in Ohio, Arizona, Kansas, Florida, and five in California. Nicky did sit in for a jam session at the Matrix on August 4 that included Dino, John, Carlos Santana, and Jorma Kaukonen and Jack Casady of Jefferson Airplane, released in 2023 on the third volume of Japan's *Sweet California Sunshine* series. The band joined the Grateful Dead at San Francisco television station KQED on August 30 for "Calibration," a live event televised and also broadcast on KQED-FM. It has never been made available on home video in any format, so it's unknown whether or not Nicky took part.

The band headed out to Texas for two shows in early September, the first at the Continental Showcase in Houston on Sunday the 6th. In the next morning's edition of the Houston Chronicle, reporter Jill Melichar's review was headlined "Wet and Wild Night Provided by Quicksilver: "The air conditioners weren't working properly and when about 7,000 or 8,000 bodies are packed together, they sweat…During intermission, the scene started to resemble a rock festival in miniature. Everybody was helping with the business at hand: keeping cool, or at least comfortable. A chant with clapping accompaniment was started to pass the time and forget the heat. Then, slowly and rhythmically, Quicksilver Messenger Service began playing and temperatures were forgotten. They started, appropriately enough, with 'Have Another Hit (of Fresh Air)' from their *Just For Love* album. Quicksilver is one of the most versatile and talented rock groups on the current scene, playing a large part of the rock spectrum. Their forte is blues rock. The people at the concert also were truly amazing. In spite of the heat, they wanted to dance! Girls grabbed their long hanks of hair and held them on top of their heads and danced until they drenched the floor around them. Guys also removed their shirts and also danced. These are the true rock cultists who will endure discomfort just to hear their music. Quicksilver felt this and gave them something worth hearing under any conditions. The group came through with quality music, such as 'Pride of Man,' throughout the evening. Of course they couldn't let the night end without 'Who Do You Love?' from their second album. There was a good 20 minutes worth of this and what they did do was positively decent. They came on like a locomotive at full speed. It has been said that Quicksilver, under pressure, is a gas. Yes, truly, truly."

On October 4, Quicksilver, the Grateful Dead, Jefferson Airplane, Hot Tuna, and the New Riders of the Purple Sage all convened at Winterland for a sold-out evening being broadcast by KQED television and could also be heard in quadraphonic stereo on radio stations KSAN and KQED. Nearly 8,000 concertgoers were packed into the ballroom and approximately 3,000 were not allowed in. What should have been a joyous replay of the spirit of '67 was spoiled considerably by the death of Janis Joplin in Los Angeles. Paul Baratta, the concert promoter, attempted to prevent the news from reaching Jefferson Airplane and Quicksilver, who had yet to hit the stage, but they had heard rumors, which were confirmed after the show. Joplin's death so depressed the Airplane's Marty Balin that he skipped the next night's performance.

For the two Winterland shows, Quicksilver replaced Nicky with Paul Butterfield's keyboard player Mark Naftalin, who would join them in the studio for the next three albums. The band augmented their sound with a five-piece horn section, including Mother Earth's Martine Fierro, which would also add a different flavor to the second album started in Hawaii. Unfortunately, the brass arrangements were hastily thrown together and unrehearsed, resulting in a set that was predictably subpar at times.

October 5 would also prove to be John's last official gig with Quicksilver, though no one, including John, knew it at the time. "I just wanted to try some new stuff," he remembered, "and a lot of the new material didn't give me much to do. Besides, I wanted to branch out. Quicksilver Messenger's Service format seemed old." Just as Dino had objected to David hanging around with the Grateful Dead, he didn't want John to play with other bands. Like Nicky, John wanted to "...do more studio work, and Quicksilver started giving me a hard time about it. They said 'If you want to do session work, you can't stay,' so I started doing sessions." Before leaving the band, he and the rest of the group—minus Dino—entered the studio in early November to finish his final instrumental piece, "Local Color." He told Rolling Stone he was "...going to produce an album by Jim Murray—he was in Quicksilver a long time ago, before we recorded. I guess I'll be playing music myself, too; it seems I can't get away from it...I was picking up on Hawaiian slack-key guitar, and I've been getting into that." He advised David to quit the group; David said he'd try to stick it out for another year.

On Sunday, November 15, Dino, David, Gary, Greg, their wives and/or girlfriends, and children prepared to fly back to Hawaii for a vacation that was Dino's latest brainstorm. Not only was John no longer a part of the organization, Ron Polte was tired of the turmoil Dino was causing and had turned management over to his brother Frank. Preparing to embark from San Francisco International Airport, equipment manager George Bonney was responsible for the postponement of the vacation, "...after an anti-hijack metal detector picked up eight bullets in Bonney's pockets," reported the November 17 edition of the San Francisco Chronicle under the headline "Quicksilver Trio Arrested—Pot." "Deputy United States Marshal James William Stafford said he searched Bonney's handbag and found 50 rifle bullets. When the marshal began a search of Bonney's person, according to police reports yesterday, Bonney fled, sprinkling the contents of a plastic bag as he ran. Stafford quickly caught the musician and Bonney allegedly told him he had a pistol in another bag and a rifle in his instrument case already aboard the plane. The pilot of the Hawaii-bound United Air Lines jet then ordered all baggage of the three men taken from the plane. A search of the bags, according to deputies, revealed no weapons but did turn up evidences of marijuana. The three musicians are scheduled to be arraigned in South San Francisco Municipal Court on November 30." Also arrested were David and conga player Jose G. Reyes, who along with Bonney were released on $1,250 bail each." (To no one's surprise, Dino's uncompromising nature ensured the Hawaiian holiday on the island of Kauai a couple weeks later was no return to paradise. It ended after only a few days. No one complained.)

In keeping with Quicksilver's occasionally confused history, complicated by sources often disagreeing on dates and events, it is highly questionable that the band's outdoor daytime performance at Sonoma State College in California took place on December 6, although two unofficial concert lists state that it did. Both John and Nicky are clearly visible in the film that exists. Further clouding the issue is the fact that December 6 was the night 200 Public Broadcasting stations aired the Ralph J. Gleason hour-long documentary "San Francisco: Go Ride the Music"—which included footage allegedly shot that day in Sonoma! (All the proof this author needs that Quicksilver did not play in Sonoma then is a reference to seeing the show in a journal kept at the time.) To make the matter even more bewildering, the DVD released in 2008 reveals that all the performances—including Jefferson Airplane's—were shot in 1969, which is most likely true. At any rate, the band is heard doing "Warm Red Wine" (an overly reverberated studio recording played as the camera pans over an empty landscape), "Baby, Baby," "Subway," and "Mona." Intercut with the live footage are scenes of the band backstage somewhere, the San Francisco cityscape, the road crew setting up the equipment, the crowd dancing, and sped up visuals of highway scenery.

For the record, the same DVD includes Gleason's 1968 documentary "West Pole," originally broadcast the following year and containing a video for "Dino's Song," the camera cutting from a shot of the moon to houseboats and the band walking around the boatyard (most likely in Larkspur) and concert scenes.

What's not in dispute is the First Annual New Year's Eve Costume Ball that took place at San Francisco's Kabuki Theatre, with John sitting in. It would be a full year before he played again with his former band mates. A two-disc recording of the concert was released by Charly/Artistry/Snapper in 2007, most of the usual suspects ("Fresh Air," "Mona," "Subway," "Pride of Man," "Mojo") among the eighteen selections as well as such new numbers as "Song For Frisco," "Doctor Feelgood," and the blues standard "You're Gonna Need Somebody On Your Bond," mistakenly listed as "Band."

Quicksilver's fifth album, *What About Me*, was finally in stores in late 1970, a productive yet strenuous and tension-filled year. It charted on January 23 and topped out at #26, one position higher than *Happy Trails* and *Just For Love*, one lower than *Shady Grove*. Dino's title song was backed with his "Good Old Rock and Roll" on a single that made it to only #100, fifty-one places less than "Fresh Air."

Unlike *Just For Love*, the latest effort was not treated kindly by the critics, one anonymous reviewer writing, "Despite some interesting piano and guitar work by Nicky Hopkins and John Cipollina respectively, the new Quicksilver LP is dragged down beyond recovery by Dino Valenti's boring vocals. He sounds like he could use a bit of clean air, if you know what I mean." Stereo Review lamented that the band was no longer "...the last word in mind-altering rock: layer upon layer of sound, nerve-wracking volume, and hostile, predatory performances." Again, the only tracks singled out for faint praise were Nicky's "Spindrifter" and John's "Local Color." As for the rest of the album, Gary and Dino's Latin-flavored "All In My Mind" was labeled "bossa olda," the writer going on to say the band seemed determined to revive the bossa nova, "...an offshoot of jazz and sticky-fingered rock" that "isn't able to provide the expertise needed for the music. Retread bossa nova just *may* be in the future, but not, I am sure, through efforts like this one." Rolling Stone's Ben Edmonds was especially harsh. While he conceded that "...the group has polished up considerably—at times nearly to the point of respectability..." he found their sound "amateurish," "half-realized," "muddled," and the "...production and engineering still far from acceptable." He continued: "The question as to whether Quicksilver now exists merely as a vehicle for the rambling romanticism of Dino Valenti is once more made unavoidable." On the plus side, he felt "What About Me" was a possible hit, and even liked "All In My Mind" as well as

"Local Color" and "Spindrifter." Despite the uniqueness of *Shady Grove* and the many attributes of *Just For Love*, Edmonds made the highly debatable claim that the last time the band made "...a statement of full musical sustenance" was the first side of *Happy Trails.*

Robert Christgau of the Village Voice, who found favor with *Just For Love* less than six months before, changed his tune regarding *What About Me*, delivering a thumbs-down verdict to the title track, "Subway," "All In My Mind," and "Call On Me," the seven-plus minute album closer: "From the self-righteous 'political' singalong to the putdown of New York to the phony samba to the horny production number, this is what people don't like about hippies. Another thing they don't like about hippies is that Dino Valenti is a hippie."

The cover of the album, which had been recorded at four different studios, was by Mike Cantrell, chiefly responsible for the *Just For Love* jacket. Once again a gatefold package, it depicted Victorian mansions sailing across the San Francisco skyline complete with symbolic trolley cars. A drawing of a guitarist stood in the shadows of the front porch, and a figure who appeared to be Gary was shown in the attic window, the only actual photograph used. The heads of the band members are rather crudely drawn on the back, flames rising from David's head. Inside, the credits included Nicky's piano on six tracks, Mark Naftalin's on three. Additional musicians: Jose Rico Reyes (conga, percussion, vocals) and the four-man horn section (Martine Fierro, Ron Taormina, Frank Morin, Pat O'Hara, Ken Balzell). Engineers: Dan Healy, Ken Hopkins, Bob Shoemaker, Peter Liebes, and the Capitol staff. Roadies: George Bonney, Doug

McGuire, and the Grateful Dead's Steve Parrish. Producer: John Palladino. Managers: Frank Polte and George Smith.

The length of *What About Me* is nearly forty-six minutes, exceeding the maximum amount for the best fidelity of vinyl by six minutes. Not helping this loss of quality sound is the frequently thin mix and over-reverberated tracks. The title song, Dino's litany of social and political ills, protests water and air pollution, deforestation, pesticides, a dishonest press, the dismissal of youth's concerns, the penal system, the military (with a reference to the Kent State massacre), and antiquated rules and regulations. He recommends taking a stand and calls for a revolution, describing himself as an outlaw on the run. It's actually a reasonably accurate seven-minute snapshot of America circa 1970, embellished by flute and horns and set to a Latin-style beat, recorded without John on October 8, a few days after his final official live appearance with the band. "Local Color," his instrumental cut in November—without Dino—benefits from improved depth on the Culture Factory edition, though Nicky is somewhat faint in the mix. It was John's last recording session with the band until 1975. Dino's "Baby Baby," the echo on his voice toned down for a change, features tasteful backup vocals, good piano from Mark Naftalin, and nice slide work by John. David's sole number, the jaunty countrified "Won't Kill Me," and his first opportunity to step forward since *Shady Grove*, also turned out to be the last time he would be singled out on a Quicksilver album. John's slide and Nicky's jangling key work elevate this lighthearted moment to something more than mere filler. "Long Haired Lady," another moody Dino ballad in the same vein as the previous album's "Gone Again" and many of the tracks on his 1968 solo album, is not quite as affecting as those recordings, but is evidence of his undeniably imaginative and even captivating songwriting. Whatever else wants to criticize about Dino's dictatorial and creative dominance of the band, a lack of talent was not one of his shortcomings. He at last had a chance for real success after a decade of toil, and he was determined to make the most of it. A lot of musicians prefer playing live to the tedium of the studio, but Dino was not one of them, driven to be the best he could be on all occasions. If nothing else, he gave Quicksilver their widest exposure on the national airwaves via "Fresh Air" and "What About Me," which were still being played on classic rock stations well into the 1980s. His high, powerful voice is not particularly versatile, but is perfectly suited to such compositions like "Gone Again" and "Long Haired Lady." The second side starts with Dino and Gary's "Subway," chronicling their wasted time in New York and a Quicksilver standard that the band had been playing for the past year. John and Gary's guitar mesh as they always had, though the former's is low in the mix at times. Nicky's peaceful, nostalgic "Spindrifter," his final contribution, is serene yet powerful, with Greg's muted percussion and David's subtle bass perfectly underscoring the performance. Gary, however, felt that just Nicky and "his overdubbed piano parts" didn't require any accompaniment. "I wanted to leave it alone because it was beautiful." As for Dino's "Good Old Rock And Roll," another selection from the Hawaiian sessions suffering from an excess of echo, the best thing about it is some interplay between John and Nicky that could have led to some intriguing in-concert jamming. Its brittle sound aside, the "bossa nova" track "All In My Mind" by Gary and Dino is perhaps the album's most commercial moment, featuring a good solo by Gary, piano by Nicky, and intricate bass from either David or Gary. *What About Me* ends with Dino's "Call On Me," a potentially solid seven-and-a-half minute warhorse that goes on too long and is not very well recorded. The brass is too harsh, and the mix cluttered, the guitars and piano struggling to be heard. At least one critic at the time suggested that the better tracks should have been combined with the best of *Just For Love* to make up one outstanding album. Different strokes for different folks…

*

"Quicksilver was undeniably good. The band had a seemingly endless repertoire of excellent songs, delivered with polish and spirit."

The Seattle Times, 02-13-71

The seemingly endless war in Vietnam slogged along despite Nixon's vow in 1968 to end it. At least the number of American troops dropped to 140,000, Lt. William Calley, Jr., was found guilty of murder for the My Lai massacre, and the *New York Times* exposed the truth about the government's expansion of the war when it published the Pentagon Papers. The People's Republic of China was admitted to the U.N. and Taiwan was booted out. Eighteen-year-olds were given the right to vote, and the Supreme Court finally supported the integration of public schools. Vitamin B12 was synthesized, phosphates in detergents were determined to cause water pollution, and astronomers discovered two new galaxies near the Milky Way.

The era of the singer/songwriter continued during the new year, many of the most popular albums the product of solo artists, some releasing career peaks: John Lennon's *Imagine*, Carole King's *Tapestry*, Rod Stewart's *Every Picture Tells A Story*, Marvin Gaye's *What's Going On*, and David Crosby's mesmerizing *If I Could Only Remember My Name*, which one review called "a landmark of West Coast tripping." (With David Freiberg sitting in.) The top bands were all British: Led Zeppelin's fourth, Jethro Tull's *Aqualung*, the Rolling Stones' *Sticky Fingers,* and *Who's Next* by the Who, every one of them achieving a spot in the 100 best-selling albums of the '70s. *L.A. Woman*, The Doors' final work as a quartet, earned a Gold Record less than three weeks after singer Jim Morrison's death in Paris. The Allman Brothers' *At Fillmore East* would become one of the most-lauded concert recordings ever, earning a Gold Record only four days before slide guitar wizard Duane Allman was killed in a motorcycle accident. Like the many benefit concerts for various causes that San Francisco musicians had been playing for years, George Harrison coaxed Bob Dylan out of isolation for the Concert For Bangla Desh in August, intended to help relieve the suffering of the starving citizens in one of India's poorest regions.

The most notable music from San Francisco were the Grateful Dead's first Gold Record (a live self-titled two-record set), Santana's third, and Janis Joplin's posthumous *Pearl*, featuring her unforgettable cover version of Kris Kristofferson's "Me and Bobby McGee." Otherwise, flower power was fading: the Steve Miller Band's *Rock Love* was their weakest to date, Country Joe & the Fish were MIA, and Jefferson Airplane—still existing in two camps, with Grace Slick and Paul Kantner in one, Jorma Kaukonen and Jack Casady (a/k/a Hot Tuna, who put out a second live album, this one electric)—in the other. Their 1971 effort, *Bark* (on their own Grunt label) had a couple of good moments but was disjointed and not much livelier than the dead fish on the cover. In November Quicksilver released an album simply titled *Quicksilver*, which today remains a favorite among the band's most fervent fans. It first hit the sales charts on December 4 and was their most disappointing effort yet in commercial terms, stalling at #114 even though its sound quality was an improvement over the previous two recordings and contained stronger material. The band, still capable of drawing huge crowds, blamed the dismal sales on their label. "We didn't sell a lot of records like some of the other groups," said Gary, "and Capitol Records is not noted for promoting their acts and they didn't promote us. We could make a new record and nobody would even know it." It would not be the last time Gary complained about the company, which had such major artists as the Beatles, Beach Boys, Grand Funk Railroad, Steve Miller, Merle Haggard, Glen Campbell, and Quicksilver on its roster but still lost eight million dollars in 1970.

In June 1971, Bhaskar Menon, an EMI executive from India and London, took control of Capitol, slashing its slate of artists, cutting back on the number of promotional albums shipped, and reducing their staff on both coasts. The general consensus in the music community was that the label had become overly dependent on the Beatles, and did not have much of a relationship with the rock press. Rumors began circulating that the Steve Miller Band and Quicksilver Messenger Service were going to be dropped if their sales did not improve considerably.

After taking January off, Quicksilver Messenger Service filled 1971 with no less than fifty shows, more than 1969 and 1970 combined, Gary now the only lead guitarist. Their first date, in Seattle, drew a crowd of nearly four thousand to a benefit for a fourth annual Sky River rock festival. According to reporter Janine Gressel, the masses were initially unruly due to the concert's delay but "… Quicksilver quickly dispelled the mood and made a solid hit with the audience. The band was in fine form, playing for a long (one hour and 45 minutes) and satisfying concert." A cursory check of newspaper archives across the nation and elsewhere confirms that the band was greeted enthusiastically throughout the year, playing in Vancouver, Connecticut, Washington DC, Ohio, Tennessee, Georgia, Missouri, Kansas,

Oklahoma, Wisconsin, Minnesota, Illinois, Colorado, Louisiana, Texas, Florida, Arizona, Nebraska, Michigan, and, of course, California. On March 5 and 6 they played New York's Fillmore East for the fifth and final time. With Jefferson Airplane gradually falling apart, the only San Francisco groups to extensively spread their music during the year were Quicksilver and the Grateful Dead.

In April, the Milwaukee Sentinel reported: "Quicksilver Messenger Service, a musical powerhouse with five tons of amplifiers, created its biggest sensation of the night with its stormy 20-minute-long 'Who Do You Love.' The Service's performance was filled with exciting moments, many of them brought on by the cajolery of the voices and guitars of Dino Valenti and Gary Duncan. After the group finished its set, the crowd became clamorous and refused to budge from its seats and clear the theater for the second show until Service gave an encore."

Two months later, a bold headline in the Houston Chronicle trumpeted, "Quicksilver Fine In Coliseum Show," staff writer John W. Wilson reporting: "It's been about three years since all that rock and roll came out of the sunshine state, but there are still some of the groups who made it all possible, and one of them, Quicksilver Messenger Service, came into the Coliseum Sunday night. It was a good night for music. The musicians came to play, and the people came to participate. Quicksilver was fine. They reminded you of the halcyon days of 1967-68 when peace and turning-on were the bywords of that strange generation from the Haight." That night, with Joey Covington of Jefferson Airplane sitting in on additional percussion, the band was top-billed over ZZ Top and the Allman Brothers Band.

In May, Time magazine had reported that Bill Graham was closing the Fillmore East in Manhattan sometime in summer, followed by San Francisco's Fillmore West in the fall. The reason for shuttering what the publication referred to as "...the two cathedrals of the loud, hard-driving sound that for a memorable decade has been the soul of youth's counterculture" was Graham's feeling "...that rock had gained so much of the world that it had lost its soul." "When we started in 1965," he explained, "I associated with and employed 'musicians.' Now it's 'officers' and 'stockholders' in large corporations—only they happen to have long hair and play guitars. Rock music is becoming a General Motors, a Pacific Gas and Electric."

As it happened, the Fillmore West was scheduled to cease operations in July, not the fall. The final week—June 29 to July 4—featured twenty acts, including Boz Scaggs, It's A Beautiful Day, the Elvin Bishop Group, the Grateful Dead, the New Riders of the Purple Sage, Santana, and Creedence Clearwater Revival. Quicksilver Messenger Service was billed over Hot Tuna and the Sons of Champlin (now calling themselves Yogi Phlegm) on Saturday, July 3, performing eighteen numbers. Included were such staples as "Fresh Air," "Mona," "Subway," "Mojo," "Who Do You Love," and "What About Me" in addition to Gary's "Doin' Time in the USA," destined for their final Capitol album the next year. Also released in 1972 were the three-record box set *Fillmore: the Last Days* and a theatrical feature film of the event directed by Richard T. Heffron and released by 20th Century-Fox. Two tracks—"Fresh Air" and "Mojo"—would be on both the album and in the film. In recent years a bootleg double CD from Australia, mistakenly titled *Independence Day 1971*, made Quicksilver's entire set available. Oddly, the correct date—July 3, not the 4th—was printed on the back cover, but the front and back of the package are illustrated with photos of John, who was not there.

In reviews of Quicksilver's two numbers, one critic referred to the band as "…that dynamo of groovie vibes." Rolling Stone's Tom Nolan wrote: "Bill Graham introduces the Quicksilver Messenger Service with a little roughhouse fun. 'Some of the baddest people in the world,' assures Bill, and QMS threatens to prove it with Dino Valenti's churning 'Fresh Air.' They sound like…Santana! Their energy dissipates in the next Valenti opus, 'Mojo,' a typical Quicksilver 'your-money's worth' letdown. However, the crowd likes it. It likes everything, indiscriminately." The magazine's reaction to the documentary didn't mention Quicksilver at all in its review of the film, and all another critic said was, "Did you ever notice how much Dino Valente (sic) resembles Victor Mature?"

It is not clear precisely when David quit the band, and it's very likely the Fillmore West show was his last. Nor is it known how much he participated in the recording of the *Quicksilver* album, but he is included in seven of the black-and-white photos making up the collage on the back cover. Not helpful was his arrest for pot while the sessions were underway. When at least two tracks (Dino's "Don't Cry My Lady Love" and Gary's "Fire Brothers") were laid down between July 19 and 27, he had been replaced on bass by Mark Ryan.

Before work on the album resumed in October, Quicksilver's live dates included a raucous four nights in August at the legendary Whisky in Los Angeles, and New York's prestigious Carnegie Hall in September.

Quicksilver was released in November to slow sales and largely half-hearted reviews, Rolling Stone's Patrick Carr declaring, "*Quicksilver* is Dino Valenti's album" and that it contained only good two songs—Dino's "Hope" and "I Found Love" by Gary, whom he erroneously indentified as the band's drummer. He also stated that John was still a member of the group. Though Dino's penchant for infusing practically everything with echo had been toned down, Carr complained that "…this persistent feature serves only to mask what might have been attractive ballads" and felt only one cut—"Rebel"—profited from it. Damning with faint praise, he concluded, "It grieves me to say this, since I'll take Quicksilver's good intentions and real glow-power potential over a hundred hoarily decadent Phase Four evil-rock bands, but Quicksilver is mediocre, and ain't that a shame?" Rock magazine's Frank Fillchock was even more blunt, starting his critique by stating, "I hate Dino Valenti!" and lamenting, "The truth is that Quicksilver is a pale shadow of its former self—listless, pedestrian, drained of the energies which sustained it through San Francisco's golden era. As that bright dream folded, apparently so have they." Both critics obviously opted to long for the good, old days of 1967-68 rather than consider the album in the context of the musical climate of 1971. Times change, sounds change, bands change—or they become dated, irrelevant. In reality, Quicksilver Messenger Service was still high-energy and a guaranteed concert attraction. Capitol's failure to capture them live on vinyl was a missed opportunity, and this author, a regular consumer of music publications back in the day, can testify that the *Quicksilver* album suddenly appeared in record racks with no advance notice. Its present-day reputation among the band's admirers as regrettably unappreciated is due to its discovery long after the fact. (Significantly, when Capitol issued its first compilation of Quicksilver's recordings in 1973, there were more tracks from *Quicksilver*—four—than any other album.) No doubt little remembered now is this interesting bit of trivia: The same month the album was released, Rolling Stone's Jon Tiven, in his negative review of Bo Diddley's *Another Dimension*, remarked that Quicksilver was "…more into the Bo Diddley thing than Bo is. And they're trying hard to get into it while he's doing his best to get away from it. Yeah, Quicksilver's better at being Bo Diddley than Bo Diddley is, at least for the moment."

Quicksilver's cover art was painted by Burray Olson and depicted a giant hawk rising above a wolf and two semi-naked longhairs, the imagery quite possibly inspired by the lyrics of Gary's "Fire Brothers." This time there was no gatefold packaging and the credits were in tiny print on the back cover, listing the songs and their composers, but no information about the musicians responsible. In his review, Rock's Fillchock disclosed that, "It took a 30-minute call to the Coast to determine that the present make-up is Valenti, Duncan, Greg Ellmore (sic) on drums and David Friedberg (sic) on bass, with Mark Naftalin sitting in on keyboards." Capitol made no mention of new bass player Mark Ryan, David's permanent replacement. The album was probably self-produced as no one was given credit.

Opening *Quicksilver* is Dino's "Hope," a sequel of sorts to "What About Me" in that it concerns the younger generation getting wise to the older generation's failings. It's an anthem with a galloping pace, Greg's drums better recorded than usual. The multiple guitars are obviously overdubbed to compensate for the loss of John. Gary's "I Found Love" was chosen as the single, backed with "Hope," and failed to dent the sales chart or garner decent airplay. His double-tracked confessional (how love rescued him from drug abuse) is his strongest vocal to date and chugs along backed by both organ and piano. Dino joins in on the final chorus, reminiscent of the Beatles' "All You Need is Love." The potentially annoying wah-

wah pedal of Gary's guitar is, thankfully, used judiciously on Dino's "Song For Frisco," on which he pines for the past glories of the city. Mark Naftalin's piano is prominent, the organ understated. Dino's vocal on "Play My Guitar" is, refreshingly, not saturated in reverb, and he once again refers to being thought "crazy." The bass sounds like David's style, so it's possible this is one of the few tracks he may have contributed to. "Rebel," evidently told from the viewpoint of a Confederate veteran, features backup vocals that are nothing more than a cacophony of war whoops and, yes, rebel yells; the most negligible cut on the album. Gary's "Fire Brothers" is essentially a duet between his subdued acoustic guitar and Naftalin's dramatic piano, the arpeggios strongly reminiscent of Nicky's flourishes. Gary's vocal can only be described as effectively ghostly. Just as *Shady Grove* was largely David's album, *Quicksilver* was the first album to place Gary's skills as a singer, composer, and musician at the forefront. Dino's "Out of My Mind," like many of his songs, seems to be autobiographical, a ballad not excessively echoed. The acoustic guitar and tambourine are accompanied by an interesting, active bass played by either David or Mark Ryan. Mark Naftalin is the "star" of Dino's bouncy, wistful "Don't Cry My Lady Love," overdubbed to sound like two pianos. (He was inducted into the Rock & Roll Hall of Fame in 2015 as part of the Paul Butterfield Blues Band.) The acoustic ballad is underscored by a simple, non-intrusive bass. Closing this, arguably the best of the four Quicksilver albums from the Valenti era, is the seven-minute "The Truth," which the band had been playing live for well over a year and explains why it is conceivably David on bass. The slashing wah-wah guitar drives this ambitiously loping number, its highlight an impressive organ break. And Dino repeats his bugaboo about being judged "crazy."

While David was no longer in the band when *Quicksilver* was completed, he was anything but idle, nor was John. Both assisted Mickey Hart, one of the Grateful Dead's drummers, in recording his first solo album, *Rolling Thunder*, which would be released the following year. John contributed guitar to four of the ten tracks, David five, adding vocals, bass, piano, viola, and even assisting Dan Healy, Mickey, and two others with engineering.

Much of November and December was spent on initial sessions for the next album, live dates severely cut back mainly because cost conscious Capitol allegedly refused to help promote their concerts and had not shared any of the band's expenses for the summer and fall tour. According to Quicksilver's contract, their deal with the label extended to the end of 1972, by which time they were obligated to record three more albums. As they began work on what would be known as *Comin' Thru* there was no indication that it would be their last.

Quicksilver closed out 1971 at the Friends and Relations Hall in San Francisco's Playland Amusement Park for the second annual New Year's Eve Costume Ball, supported by Big Brother & the Holding Company, Stoneground, and Sopwith Camel. As he had for the final night of 1970, John made a surprise return, playing with Big Brother and joining Quicksilver for the encore.

*

1972-1977

"According to lead guitarist Gary Duncan, Quicksilver is going through a 'transitory period,' mainly because of all the trouble they've been having with their label. Due to financial trouble, Capitol is cutting corners and Quicksilver seems to be getting the short end of the stick."

Rock, 1972

Nixon visited China and became the first president to go to Moscow. His cronies were arrested for breaking into the Watergate headquarters of the Democratic National Committee, but the crime was temporarily covered up and he was re-elected anyway. The actions of Arab terrorists result in fifteen deaths at the Munich Olympics. The Equal Employment Opportunity Act required the same hiring practices for both sexes, and the country's gross national product reached $1 trillion.

In the estimation of some music historians, 1972 was the peak year of the Seventies, the last time there was an overwhelming abundance of excellent albums: *Rock of Ages* (The Band), *Gumbo* (Dr. John), *Eagles*, *I'm Still in Love With You* (Al Green), *Everybody's in Showbiz* (The Kinks), *For the Roses* (Joni Mitchell), *St. Dominic's Preview* (Van Morrison), *Something/Anything* (Todd Rundgren), *Exile On Main Street* (The Rolling Stones), *Manassas* (Stephen Stills), *Never A Dull Moment* (Rod Stewart), *Talking Book* (Stevie Wonder), and numerous others that have stood the test of time.

As for San Francisco's musical luminaries, the Jefferson Airplane's final studio album, *Long John Silver*, was an improvement over the previous year's *Bark*. Hot Tuna's *Burgers* was their first studio recording and best to date. Santana launched a monumental jazz/rock trilogy with *Caravanserai*. The Steve Miller Band released the underrated *Recall the Beginning...A Journey From Eden.* The Grateful Dead, more popular than ever, undertook their hugely successful tour of Europe, memorialized on a three-record set the following year. Creedence Clearwater Revival, the most prolific and popular Bay

Area band, wisely called it a day with *Mardi Gras,* their weakest album. In April, Quicksilver Messenger Service's seventh Capitol album hit the racks with a thud, climbing no farther than #134, twenty positions lower than *Quicksilver* and their most commercially unsuccessful.

In January, the band replaced pianist Mark Naftalin with organist Chuck Steaks, who would remain in the lineup for the next two years and join the sessions for the album already in progress. (John and his first post-Quicksilver band, Copperhead, performed live on San Francsico's KSAN-FM on the 23rd.) The band spent the latter part of the month playing gigs in Connecticut, New Jersey, New York, Georgia, Louisiana, and Florida, where a show for a crowd of nearly four thousand in Tampa on the last night of the month did not go smoothly. After playing a typically long set which had gone into overtime, the band responded to the audience's cries for an encore and returned to the stage. The venue's manager went ballistic and threatened to cut the power. Ignoring Gary's recommendation that they skip "What About Me" and leave, Dino replied, "I don't care if I have to run through the jungle in the middle of the night, I'm gonna play that song!" Which they did. The police were called and arrested the singer backstage for inciting a riot and profanity. Dino was released after bond was posted, telling the press that Florida had, "The worst cops I've ever seen." When the band arrived in West Palm Beach a couple of days later, they discovered that the police there had been warned about what occurred in Tampa and were ready for trouble. Dino's opinion of Florida law enforcement wasn't changed by the sight of the officers beating a disruptive member of the audience. The band beat a hasty retreat and was greeted by the sight of several policemen surrounding their limousine. They hitched a ride with a pair of young women, whose car almost immediately had a flat tire. That necessitated an escape across a golf course—on foot in a thunderstorm—to their hotel. Dino did indeed end up running through the jungle after all. After sneaking up to their rooms—"like a commando raid," said Dino—they packed their bags, checked out, and went down the road to a Holiday Inn, narrowly eluding several police cars that pulled up with sirens screaming. Back at the concert hall, conga player Harold Aceves, formerly one of the band's roadies, had exited the building before the other musicians and was arrested. The innocent local limo driver was cited for conspiracy.

A two-night date at Winterland was their only chronicled date in February, and March included only one appearance. April, however, found them across the pond for a show at the London School of Economics on the 28th, after which Mark Ryan was out as bassist and Roger Stanton was in.

An untrue rumor that the band was leaving Capitol for Warner Bros. circulated in the recording industry just as *Comin' Thru* was released. In fact Capitol allowed them to have another gatefold cover for the album, drawn once again by Burray Olson (misspelled "Burry" in the credits, which also indentify Dino's congas as "cungas") and depicting a few longhaired maidens—one topless—amid a rising sun with facial features, a grounded hawk, five charging equines—one a unicorn—and a night sky in which a cloud with a face blows a gale of wind. Inside are three separate portraits of the four band members, all linked to resemble a twelve-man army, standing beside a boatyard pole stamped with a 7, obviously a reference to this album's number. While there is no information as to where or exactly when it was recorded, the horn section is named and had grown from five players used on *What About Me* to seven.

The rock press was not kind, one review simply saying, "See what I mean? I would never buy this. Horns!" ignoring the reality that rock music had included horns since its earliest days. In recent years horns had been used by the Beatles, the Stones, Santana, Jefferson Airplane, Janis Joplin, Van Morrison, Chicago, and Blood, Sweat & Tears in particular. And there were horns on Quicksilver's debut in 1968. Circus magazine said the band was "…rockin' and rollin' with all the oomph of a ruptured carrier pigeon" and "…packs all the wallop of a case of terminal sleeping sickness." Dino was branded as "…the master of rock egocentricity" while Rolling Stone's Mike Saunders remarked, "Dino Valenti had a pretty good niche in history carved out for a while" as the writer of "'Get Together,' one of the best things to come out of the whole Summer of Love" but then "… went and ruined it all by joining Quicksilver, and pretty well ruining them." This from a "fan" who admitted he didn't even care for *Happy Trails*. Oh? Tell me how you *really* feel… Just what the public needs: reviews by critics who don't even care for their subjects in the first place, rather than someone who can be reasonably unbiased, such as Arthur Levy's level-headed critique in the May 1972 issue of Zoo World, its cover a reproduction of the new album's artwork, which balanced honest criticism of the album's shortcomings with acknowledgments of what there was to admire.

Long considered the nadir of Quicksilver's recorded legacy, *Comin' Thru*, like many albums seen as disappointments when first released, actually holds up rather well today. It's the sound of human beings playing real instruments and putting out a lot of natural energy without artifice. One can certainly have their own reaction to the quality of the material, but the sincerity of the delivery can't be denied. If forced to choose, the overall impact of *What About Me* is less satisfying than *Comin' Thru*. As the Who's Pete Townsend said in his 1980 song "Jools and Jim," anyone can have an opinion. Once again, different strokes for different folks. Some music freaks just don't dig change or variety.

The first cut, Gary's "Doin' Time in the USA," is easily the most commercial and sounds like it could have been at least a marginal hit like "Fresh Air" or "What About Me," propelled by Mark Ryan's rollicking bass, Chuck Steaks' heavy organ, and a Santana-style guitar. Dino joins Gary on vocals, referencing the Rolling Stones' "Satisfaction" in the process. "Chicken" is so obviously inspired by Dylan's "Subterranean Homesick Blues" or perhaps Chuck Berry's "Too Much Monkey Business" that the writing credit reads "Traditional Arrangement by D. Valenti." For once his raspy vocal is not drenched in reverb, and the sax and trombone are accompanied by Steaks' effective organ swells. Dino's "Changes," a lament over lost love, features flute (and horns), and the only use of the piano on the album. Ryan's bass is more prominent than the guitars, but not to the song's detriment. "California State Correctional Facility Blues" hearkens back to "Look Over Yonder Wall/State Farm" on the 1969/70 *Castles in the Sand* disc. The band pulls out all the stops on what could have been a live, free-form studio jam with only guitar overdubs, highlighted by Greg's furious drumming, Gary's bluesy guitar, and Chuck's "busy" organ. Some lyrics of Dino's rough, aggressive vocal may very well be improvised. Side Two is the most cohesive, nonstop onslaught of sound since the first side of *Happy Trails* as well as the most consistently satisfying series of tracks since the second side of *Just For Love*. "Forty Days"—not the same similarly titled songs by Muddy Waters and Steppenwolf—strikes a good balance between wailing guitars and horns, Dino's echoed vocal appropriately effective rather than irritating. Greg and Mark provide a rock solid base. "Mojo," which the band had been performing in concert for over two years, has finally been captured in the studio, with horns (including a screaming trumpet) added. Everything drops out for a bass solo, the other instruments coming back one-by-one. "Don't Lose It," a vaguely political number co-written by Dino and Gary, features organ and guitar breaks and a solo vocal by Gary before the jazzy conclusion. All in all a dose of adrenaline. It's not clear who they're advising to hang on, though one hopes it wasn't Nixon, whom Crawdaddy magazine claimed was supported by Dino.

Following a light concert schedule in May, ping-ponging between Virginia and New Jersey, Quicksilver hit the road in June for a summer tour of at least fifteen dates that included Summerfest in Milwaukee, Wisconsin, on Sunday, July 23, the first time this author heard them live. Fortunately, I was keeping a journal at the time and made this entry: "What a fantastic evening. Although they were cut off after an hour and fifteen minutes because they were running over, Quicksilver played a great set. Dino Valenti is really a likable showman. At one point he said the show was 'a gas,' which it was, and I felt sorry when the fair people said to quit. They were pissed and Dino threw his mike stand down. Anyway, they did 'Fresh Air,' 'Baby Baby,' 'Doin' Time in the USA,' 'The Hat,' 'Mojo,' 'Mona,' and some new stuff. It was during 'Who Do You Love' that they were cut off so the Doors could come on at 11:00." Gary later said they suspected the manager or one of the Doors had unplugged their equipment while mid-song and had hit the member of Quicksilver's crew who tried to restore power.

The band dared to return to Florida for shows in Miami, Orlando, Pensacola, and yes, Tampa, site of the January fiasco. In August, David officially joined the limping Jefferson Airplane, and Quicksilver continued promoting *Comin' Thru*, returning to Wisconsin and Florida as well as Pennsylvania, Ohio, Virginia, and New York's Central Park. A September date in England was canceled, and an October 13 show at the Academy of Music was curiously billed as a "Farewell Performance." It wasn't, but a November appearance in North Carolina was canceled, as was a two-night stand in December at Winterland. Details of possible trouble brewing behind the scenes were not known, but Chuck Steaks told a reporter their tours were "weird" and that airlines gave them a hard time when they attempted to keep their guitars with them to avoid being damaged instead of stowing them in the baggage department.

Quicksilver's relationship with their label was not improving, although they still had artistic control over the content and packaging of their albums. In addition to scaling back on promotion and not chipping in on touring expenses, Capitol would not loan the band some pieces of sound equipment. The group had to purchase their own. When Gary was interviewed by a now long-defunct music rag, he claimed, "When *Comin' Thru* received some bad reviews when it was first released, Capitol withheld any promotion that they might have intended for the group."

Lewis Segal, National Publicity Manager for Capitol, said he was "puzzled" by Gary's negative assessment. "First off," he responded, "marketing plans and advertising support for albums are determined far in advance of release day, so by the time those catastrophic bad reviews appeared, virtually all of the promotion lavished (as you shall see) on *Comin' Thru* had been spent. Next, think about this: is the record company that promoted Grand Funk when they were the rock press' pet hate likely to fall apart over a few bad reviews over Quicksilver? In point of fact, the only thing 'withheld' from Quicksilver promotion because of bad reviews was advertising in a certain national music magazine—and that specifically at the group's request. Otherwise, Quicksilver advertising appeared in twenty-eight college papers, as well as *Billboard, Fusion, The Chicago Seed, The Staff, The Los Angeles Free Press, Night Times, Circus, The Village Voice,* and *Rock*. In addition, about eight thousand dollars was spent on FM radio buys, a new publicity biography was prepared, and some twelve thousand kites reproducing the *Comin' Thru* album cover were manufactured and distributed. (For Quicksilver's previous LP, we had sent out patches. In short, if Capitol *had* 'refused to promote Quicksilver,' they could have found a cheaper way to do it."

Greg told the press they had as many as six songs prepared for their next album, and were thinking of recording it live in a rehearsal hall. That would turn out to be wishful thinking. The two albums the band still owed Capitol would ultimately turn out to be a two-record compilation of previously released tracks, which Greg obviously had no way of knowing at the time.

There would be no New Year's Eve celebration concert in 1972, but the night before they performed in my hometown, Rockford, Illinois, at the National Guard Armory. As I noted in my journal: "Well, I saw Quicksilver again tonight and it was really fine. Flash and Blue Oyster Cult were good, but my #1 fave took top honors, of course. Aside from Dino getting ticked off because his mike didn't work during 'The Hat,' it was a nice, smooth show. They did a new, fast blues called 'Dr. Feelgood,' 'Fresh Air,' 'Mojo,' 'Mona,' 'Who Do You Love,' 'Play My Guitar,' 'Baby Baby,' 'Doin' Time in the U.S.A.,' and then came back and did 'What About Me' and 'Freeway Flyer.' Dino had us sing the chorus of 'What About Me' (I was loud and hoppin'), let a black guy play congas, and shook hands with the front row. I sure would have liked to have been up front! I tried to get backstage, but all except Greg Elmore (I got about 20 feet from him) had left." What I didn't mention was that the armory, including a balcony that ran along one side, was packed to capacity by several hundred excited fans. Before the show, two attractive, long-haired blonde young women appeared to be with Dino, who, like Gary, wore a red shirt. As for getting so near to Greg, I approached the stage, which was only a few feet high, and flashed him the peace sign. The stage lights went off, but he remained seated behind his drums, sweating and breathing heavily. He smiled and nodded. "Great show!" I said. He nodded again and replied, "Thanks, man. I'm beat!"

Coincidentally, the friend I attended the concert with was, of course, a Quicksilver fan who eerily resembled Dino—short, dark-complexioned, walked with a swagger, and fancied himself a ladies' man. On one wall of his apartment he had pinned an ad for the *Quicksilver* album and a color photo of Dino from some music magazine. When he and I got together with other guys for Friday night poker games, he inevitably slapped the same music on his turntable: Johnny Winter, the Allman Brothers, the J. Geils Band, Uriah Heep, Savoy Brown, and—always—the second side of *Comin' Thru*, which he also had in his car on eight-track. One of his favorite Quicksilver tunes was "Gone Again" from *Just For Love*, which he called his "broad pleaser." Ah, gone are the days…

*

"For better than an hour Quicksilver produced a mixture of rock music, keeping the audience in a boogie mood as tune after tune exploded out of the speakers."

The Oregonian, January 27, 1973

A cease-fire agreement in Vietnam was signed in Paris, the last U.S. troops were withdrawn, and Hanoi released the prisoners of war held there. Vice President Spiro Agnew's tax evasion resulted in his resignation; he was replaced by Gerald Ford. Nixon was finally forced to release tapes revealing the Watergate cover-up. Native American protestors took over the village of Wounded Knee, where in 1890 the U.S. Cavalry had slaughtered more than 150 Sioux. The Supreme Court passed the Roe vs. Wade ruling. Gasoline shortages pointed to the coming energy crisis, and Congress approved the trans-Alaska pipeline. Airlines began screening passengers after an increase in skyjackings. New York City's World Trade Center opened. Director George Lucas, in his film *American Graffiti*, set in 1962, celebrated the pop music of the 1950s and early '60s, leading to an increased interest in the sounds and artists of those more innocent days.

In other 1973 music news, many of the artists who had released important work the previous year produced albums that suffered by comparison. Emerging performers who would only loom larger as the decade went on included Bruce Springsteen, Elton John, David Bowie, and Lynyrd Skynyrd. Rock/jazz fusion continued to be relatively healthy, particularly the Mahavishnu Orchestra's *Birds of Fire*. Progressive rock had not yet lapsed into dull noodling, as evidenced by Jethro Tull's wildly underrated gem *A Passion Play* and Pink Floyd's monumental *Dark Side of the Moon*, the fourth best-selling album of the decade. The Spinners' first album for Atlantic was destined to be their best ever, and Stevie Wonder extended his incredibly creative streak with *Innervisions*, his third major work in a row. All four former Beatles released significant albums, and the reputation of the Rolling Stones' *Goat's Head Soup*, though initially judged a disappointment after 1972's *Exile On Main Street* (which it outsold) was to grow over subsequent years, like several other efforts by the band. Steely Dan's sophomore album, *Can't Buy a Thrill*, was even better than their promising debut the year before.

The spirit of '67 was kept alive with the Grateful Dead's majestic three-record live set *Europe '72*, a tribute to the recently-deceased Rod "Pigpen" McKernan (*History of the Grateful Dead—Vol. 1—Bear's Choice)*, and *Wake of the Flood*, their first studio album in three years, released on their own label. Jefferson Airplane's swan song, the live *Thirty Seconds Over Winterland*—with Quicksilver's David joining on vocals—proved more rewarding than their last two studio efforts. David was co-billed with Paul Kantner and Grace Slick for the album *Baron von Tollbooth and the Chrome Nun*, contributing his fine composition "The Harp Tree." Santana delivered *Welcome*, arguably their greatest achievement, and Carlos Santana teamed up with the Mahavishu Orchestra's John McLaughlin to create the epochal *Love, Devotion and Surrender*. Nicky released his *The Tin Man Was a Dreamer*, with a remake of "Edward." Hot Tuna continued their line of winners with *The Phosphorescent Rat*, and Steve Miller, signed to Capitol at the same time as Quicksilver, avoided being dropped by the label when his album *The Joker* became a surprise hit. But for the first time since 1967, Quicksilver Messenger Service was without a recording contract.

Although the band owed Capitol Records two more albums, the label cut them loose and filled the void with *Quicksilver Anthology*, a marginally satisfying two-record set released in April that eventually sold in sufficient numbers to hit #108, slightly higher than either of the band's last two efforts. While its sixteen selections included such essential tracks as "Pride of Man," "Dino's Song," "Mona," "Fresh Air," and "What About Me," it dismissed "Who Do You Love," "Calvary," "Shady Grove," "Stand By Me," and everything from *Comin' Thru* in favor of the debatable "Bears" and "Three Or Four Feet From Home." The compilation was first released on CD in a two-disc set by BGO Records in 1995. Five years before that, Capitol assembled a one-disc collection they termed *The Best of Quicksilver* (reissued in 2005 with a different cover) whose eleven tracks included six that were not in the *Anthology*, wisely choosing "Who Do You Love" (single edit) from *Happy Trails*, "Shady Grove" and "Joseph's Coat" from the third album, the stand-alone single "Stand By Me," the questionable "Long Haired Lady" (instead of the superior Dino ballad "Gone Again") and "California State Correctional Facility Blues" from *Comin' Thru* (rather than the more appropriate "Doin' Time in the U.S.A.").

Music critic Robert Christgau of the *Village Voice*, whose reactions to Quicksilver in the past had been decidedly mixed, rated the *Anthology* a C+, saying "...this compilation is where they admit defeat, and why not? Neither Nicky Hopkins expressing himself nor Dino Valenti acting free—good thing (for him) that he was busted for dope rather than impersonating a vocalist or he'd still be up the river—could stop this band from dating in record time."

The *Sons of Mercury (1968-1975)* double disc from Rhino/Capitol released in 1991 remains the most representative Quicksilver compilation. It has not only their first commercially released recordings (for the *Revolution* soundtrack) but also two tracks from the 1975 reunion album. One can quibble over what was chosen and what was not, but all of the unquestionable highlights are here.

In 1999, Collectors' Choice Music/Capitol combined to issue *Unreleased Quicksilver Messenger Service: Lost Gold and Silver*, a limited two-disc edition containing the two *Revolution* cuts, live material, and studio demos that have been scattered across numerous other collections in the ensuing years.

Before re-releasing the 1990 *Best of Quicksilver* in 2005, Capitol put together *Classic Masters* in 2002, mainly the same album with one extra track ("Hope") and two substitutions ("Light Your Windows," "Flute Song" in place of "Long Haired Lady" and "California State Correctional Facility Blues"). Take your pick.

Because Quicksilver was not in the record racks until the 1975 reunion album, the general public assumed the band ceased to exist during 1973-74, which was far from true. Whereas they had put on roughly thirty shows during 1972, they nearly tripled that in 1973.

Reporter John Wendeborn, in his review of the January 27 show, wrote: "Quicksilver came to Portland's Paramount Northwest theater Friday night to play for a sellout crowd of 3,000 folks, all of whom wanted to 'boogie.' So Dino Valenti and friends obliged with enthusiasm…All in all, it was a good show. Valenti's hypersensitive activity onstage keeps the other four members of the group, organ, drums, bass, and lead guitar, from the doldrums and his vocals tried to be a key to the Quicksilver style.

That style is heavily into electricity, instrumentally, and gives Valenti the right framework to work around."

By the time they hit Kennesaw Junior College in Georgia on April 19, in support of Lynyrd Skynyrd, they had logged more than forty shows all over the country, nearly always the only act on the bill. A story in the Marietta Journal, illustrated by a photograph of the band from the inside cover of *Comin' Thru*, announced that Quicksilver was bringing along a "15,000 watt sound system used in the New Orleans Rock Festival."

In Daytona, Florida, the next night, the band gave a typically charged performance, described in the Daytona Beach News Journal by staff writer Jeffery Kahn: "Transfused with the rhythms of Quicksilver Messenger Service, Memorial Stadium became an enclave of about 2,500 dancing, decibel-charged spectators Friday night...Quicksilver took the stage, cranked up their sound and the crowd surged to its feet, clapping, dancing, stomping their feet. Quicksilver was superb. They picked the crowd up and they put it down. 'Rock and roll,' they screamed. 'Boogie for us!' 'Do you really want to rock and roll?' teased the vocalist. 'If you insist.' He gave in and the band plugged in with a burst of adrenaline. Quicksilver established an intimate rapport with the crowd, manipulating with its music the gyrating listeners. As the crowd approached exhaustion, the band would slow it down for a breather. And then, pick it back up again. Quicksilver departed the stage and the moon rose over the east stands." For once it was Buddy Miles' band that ran overtime, due to its equipment being delayed, and had the power cut off at 11:00 because of the local noise ordinance.

In mid-May Mark Ryan was replaced on bass by John Nicholas, who remained in the lineup for the rest of the year, including another successful gig in Flint, Michigan, on June 27. Supported by two newer acts that had entered the music arena the year before—the Electric Light Orchestra and Whole Oats (later Hall & Oates)—Quicksilver, according to Brian L. Steffens of the Flint Journal, stole the show: "Wednesday night's show is likely to be known as the best rock music performance of 1973 for the Pine Knob Music Theater. There is not another grouping of rock artists or bands on the Pine Knob schedule that would indicate a rival to Quicksilver Messenger Service, Electric Light Orchestra, and Whole Oats. Quicksilver is an anachronism made good. The band flew into the rock music scene with the Jefferson Airplane back in 1967. Like many bands of that era, Quicksilver was weak on vocals, strong on 'acid rock' guitars, and appealed to a fading clan then termed 'freaks,' 'dope heads,' or 'hippies.' And the band has not changed much since. The lead vocalist is still not a good vocalist, but his stage manner has been polished and his ability to communicate with the audience is awe-inspiring. The concert was the first this year at Pine Knob where the audience overran the ushers and rangers to crowd around the stage and stay there through a two-hour set. The lead guitarist, organist, bassist and two drummers hammered out quality hard rock that rocked the house. The lead guitarist has to be one of the best in the business and the teaming of two drummers provides all the power and rhythm that the 5,000 fans could have demanded."

While it's a real shame there was never a professionally recorded live souvenir of Quicksilver in the early 1970s—and the newspaper reviews give ample proof it could have been one for the ages—their show at the Winterland Ballroom on December 1 was immortalized on both audio and videotape. Providentially, John and David joined on co-lead guitar and keyboards, respectively. Also on the keys was Bob Hogins, in place of the recently departed Chuck Steaks. The quality of the black-and-white video, issued on DVD in 2011 by Cleopatra Records in the *Anthology Box 1966-1970*, is sometimes "bleached" but still watchable. The hour-long CD, put out in 2013 by Purple Pyramid/Cleopatra, contains eight tracks, the final two blistering jams (including a snatch of John's "Cobra" from *Just For Love*) that feature freeform, jazz-inflected guitar duels between John and Gary. Even the intensity of the opening number, Ray Charles' "Losing Hand," and "Who Do You Love" is heightened by battling guitars. Dino, ever the crowd-pleaser, shines on "Play My Guitar," "Mojo," "What About Me," "The Hat" and is the same live wire I saw twice the previous year. The liner notes by Dave Thompson hit the proverbial nail on the head, as usual, when he describes "Who Do You Love" as "...a sensational performance, one to play as loud as you can bear, your heart keeping time with the manic percussion, your blood pumping hard as those garrulous guitars...you could line this version of Quicksilver's anthem with any other that you have heard them play, and there's not one that could eclipse this baby." Amen.

*

"Quicksilver Messenger Service ripped the cares of the world from a capacity Agora crowd Wednesday night with more than 90 minutes of their near-legendary brand of rebel-roarin' rock 'n' roll. True Quicksilver freaks love it."

Columbus Dispatch, December 19, 1974

Many social and cultural historians, including those devoted to music, consider 1974 the symbolic end of the Sixties, just as 1963 is often regarded as when the general mindset of the Fifties came to a close. Most symbolic was the resignation of President Nixon before he could be impeached, his fall from grace precipitated by his failed efforts to cover up the Watergate break-in. His successor, Gerald Ford, pardoned him. Ford also gave limited amnesty to Vietnam draft dodgers and military deserters. The EPA reported that smog-related deaths were as high as 4,000 per year, and aerosol sprays were suspected of depleting Earth's ozone layer. The national speed limit was capped at 55 mph in order to conserve gas while the profits of U.S. oil companies grew by more than 90 percent during the first half of the year.

Seasoned musicians and relatively newer ones, such as Wilco's Jeff Tweedy, have looked back at 1974 and judged it the end of rock's golden era. The dreaded disco beast was stalking the land, as was glitter rock, but the keepers of the flame remained firm. It was the year Dylan and the Band delivered a one-two punch with a studio album (*Planet Waves*) and a double-live set (*Before the Flood*) from their record-breaking tour. Neil Young, who along with Crosby, Stills & Nash mounted a massive stadium tour, released his enthralling *On the Beach*. Joni Mitchell's *Court and Spark* was to become the biggest commercial success of her career. After a long struggle with addiction, Eric Clapton bounced back with *461 Ocean Boulevard*, his first studio album in four years, and Joe Cocker also made a comeback with the emotionally naked *I Can Stand A Little Rain*. *Pretzel Logic*, Steely Dan's excellent fourth, was a commercial and critical success. Stevie Wonder's *Fulfillingness First Finale* was added to his wondrous series of masterworks, and Santana concluded its trilogy of adventurous jazz-influenced works with *Borboletta.*

Positive vibrations emanated from San Francisco in the form of Jefferson Starship's *Dragonfly*, with Marty Balin back in the Airplane fold and full-fledged member David co-writing the rousing "Come to Life." The Grateful Dead released *From the Mars Hotel*, the second album on their own label. Having released two albums the previous year, Hot Tuna sat the year out.

Quicksilver scaled back their activity considerably in 1974, as expenses—especially for transportation—mounted with no label support and no new product. They played less than twenty shows, and made yet another shift in personnel in February, Bob Furie taking over on bass from John Nicholas. "By 1973," said Gary, "we had changed the band lineup probably about ten times. People would come and go, and every time we got new guys the band sounded different."

Existing travelogues, often incomplete, show the band performing a solitary date in their home state (San Diego) as they stuck mainly to smaller venues in Alabama, Florida, North Carolina, Michigan, Washington, and New Jersey. One of two trips to New York included the prestigious Academy of Music, site of the Band's epic *Rock of Ages* concerts in 1971. Owing to their rightly accepted status as genuine artists, they headlined over such acts as Country Joe & the Fish, the James Gang, Tower of Power, Roy Buchanan and the Byrds' Roger McGuinn.

Ohio reporter George De Vault obviously was not up to date on the identities of the current members when reviewing their late December concert, mistaking Dino for David, John for Gary, and Bob for Gary. "Although sounding not nearly as crisp as on their albums," he wrote, "Quicksilver made up for such shortcomings with the overwhelming spirit and intensity of their music." He felt the "...soaring vocals were basically as sound as ever, but just not quite up to professional par" probably because of Dino's "three straight sleepless days (and nights) on the concert run." Otherwise, he "...more than redeemed himself with the crowd cajoling banter and power of Eric Burdon at his best. His guitar work and hoochie-coochied congas, both murder on the fingers, shook the crowd out of its December doldrums—and kept it loud." De Vault described Gary's "soul sliding lead guitar" as "fantastic" and said Bob's bass "kept things jumping." Greg—the only member accurately named—"...added even more power to the party crowd with his solid drumming." "The group's a whole passel of musical marvels wrapped up in one real tight package," he continued, "one of the few Frisco '60s sounds still hanging solidly together in the mid-'70s. Sticking mainly to newer tunes, Quicksilver easily neutralized the oppressive powers of various undercover wraiths lurking in the shadows. A crowd participation number about a cat named 'Cool Breeze' brought out the best there was to be had...'Play My Guitar' and other Quicksilver greats, plus a bit of opera and ballet sounds, completely welded those present into a single spiritual spire of rock. The super concert combination of dim lights, thick smoke and loud, LOUD music was hard at work. Quicksilver was indeed a bit of 'Fresh Air.'"

*

"Given the stature of the band during the height of the San Francisco rock scene, it is somewhat surprising that the reformation of Quicksilver Messenger Service failed to attract more interest than it has."

San Francisco Chronicle, December 30, 1975

Forces of the Viet Cong and North Vietnam took over South Vietnam as the last Americans were evacuated from Saigon. Radicals twice attempted to assassinate Gerald Ford. The energy crisis continued, and U.S. unemployment reached nearly ten percent. Director Steven Spielberg's blockbuster *Jaws* brought the curtain down on the age of offbeat, experimental American filmmaking.

In the world of music, popular acts—some more concerned with personal income than producing important work—routinely passed up comparatively intimate concert halls in favor of stadiums. With Nixon gone and the war over, it was party time in America! Disco was king, and several artists who should have known better made embarrassing stabs at incorporating it into their sound. Many of the social causes championed in the late Sixties and early Seventies began to fade from the national consciousness, as well as from a lot of the music being made, resulting in a plethora of mediocre albums. Not among them were Dylan's *Blood on the Tracks*, Jeff Beck's *Blow By Blow*, Crosby & Nash's *Wind on the Water*, Neil Young's *Tonight's the Night* and *Zuma*, Bruce Springsteen's *Born to Run*, and not many more.

From San Francisco came *Illuminations* by Carlos Santana and Alice Coltrane, the Grateful Dead's strikingly esoteric *Blues for Allah*, and Jefferson Starship's massive hit *Red Octopus* (with David's co-written "Tumblin.") John's band, Copperhead, finally released a studio album after three years together. For their fifth, *America's Choice*, Hot Tuna cranked up their amps. A major event for fans of Quicksilver Messenger Service was *Solid Silver*, the reunion album by the original members that suddenly showed up in late October on Capitol Records without much if any fanfare from the label. It charted in mid-November and made it to a respectable (for them) #89, the band's best sales position since *What About Me* reached #26 in early 1971.

Quicksilver had played only a handful of dates before entering Columbia Recording Studios in San Francisco on the last day of June to begin recording with John and David for the first time in nearly five years. "Somebody asked me if I thought we could do it," John recalled ten years later, "and I said sure…I really didn't think it would happen when I said I would do it because Freiberg was on RCA with Jefferson Starship and Dino had signed a deal with Warner Brothers and we (Copperhead) were talking about doing an album on Capitol. The reunion was fun. In a sense I was pleased with the album. It was a good representation of where we were then." David, in an interview with Bay Area historian Craig Fenton, said of the album, "It was okay. There is one track I really like, 'Gypsy Lights.' Some good came out of it. It wasn't the best work of the band…I wasn't even in the studio when the *Solid Silver* record got the final mix."

The ten tracks, completed by August 29th, were produced by the band with assistance from John Palladino, who also had not worked with them for five years. Only Gary and Greg performed on every number, John and Dino on eight, David on seven. Nicky took care of the keyboard chores on two, Michael Lewis and Jefferson Starship's Pete Sears on the rest. In addition to David (who couldn't participate in some sessions due to his commitments with Jefferson Starship), the bass chair was occupied by Skip Olson and John's brother Mario. Joining on backup vocals was Kathi McDonald, a generally unsung Bay Area blues belter with an unfairly ignored album (*Insane Asylum*) to her credit. Never at a loss for material, Dino contributed four tracks and co-wrote two others.

The front cover was a shot of the band aboard a sailboat, the familiar Quicksilver logo replaced with florid script announcing "The Original Quicksilver Messenger Service" and the album's title. The first pressing also came with a silver sticker affixed: "A brand new recording by the original Quicksilver Messenger Service featuring Gary Duncan, John Cipollina, David Freiberg, Greg Elmore, Dino Valenti." A group photo on the back cover looks as though it was taken after someone had cracked a joke, all of the members smiling or laughing. Evidently one big, happy, family, or so one would hope. In the portrait of the band on the inner sleeve, however, Dino appears to be annoyed that the other four stand with their backs to him. Open to interpretation…

Noel Coppage, critiquing the album for Stereo Review, judged the band's performance as "Very Good" and the quality of the recording "Excellent." After pointing out all the old warriors who had reconnected in recent months, he wrote, "…and now Quicksilver has put itself together again. Clearly, the Golden Age is missed. Unfortunately, it's not the kind of thing that 'getting back together' can reproduce…but it just isn't the *same*. An era passes because that's what eras do." He conceded that a few cuts ("They Don't Know," "Cowboy on the Run," "Flames") were reminiscent of "the old days without going out of style. But much of it seems to be a competent rehashing of riffs and runs endemic to an old form that just isn't slick enough for the luxury-mongering that is understandably going on in these harder times." *Rolling Stone*'s Charley Walters said the reunion was "one contradiction after another. Though much of the arranging is dull and unvaried, when the inimitable John Cipollina lets loose his stinging, tremoloed guitar, the band is at its finest." The tracks "I Heard You Singing" and "Flames" were singled out as being "rich and emotive" but called "Cowboy on the Run," one of Dino's best ballads, "a naïve flowerchild anthem." In the final analysis, Walters found the reunion a "…more personal celebration than a musical one." A decade later, in a *Goldmine* story on the band, Mick Skidmore felt the album was "patchy" and "lacked direction" but liked Gary's "Gypsy Lights" (which he regarded as the best cut) and "They Don't Know" as well as Dino's "Cowboy on the Run" and "The Letter."

Solid Silver is not the sound of a band attempting to recapture the past. More accurately, it is five old friends getting together to make music, no member overshadowing the rest. The material is varied, never dull, and well-recorded. Greg's drums are higher in the mix, the reverb is not overpowering, and everyone gets an opportunity to stand out. John plays lead on Gary's opening track, "Gypsy Lights," (the album's single) which begins with a rapid ride of Greg's drums. Gary's strong vocal is backed by Dino, David, and

Kathi McDonald, forcefully announcing that Quicksilver is indeed back. John's "HeebieJeebies," on which he plays Hawaiian steel guitar, reunites him with his close buddy Nicky Hopkins on piano. Dino's "Cowboy on the Run" is thankfully sung without excessive echo and features tasteful synthesizer by current band member Michael Lewis and Nicky on piano. (Forty years later, David covered "Cowboy" on Jefferson Starship's *Jefferson's Tree of Liberty* and in the liner notes wrote that it was one of his favorite songs by Dino. He also expressed regret that he wasn't able to be on all of *Solid Silver*'s tracks.) David's "I Heard You Singing," co-written with Grateful Dead lyricist Robert Hunter, is his sole vocal, backed by Kathi McDonald with John, Gary, and Dino on guitars. "Worryin' Shoes" is a high-voltage blues by Dino that wouldn't have been out of place on *Comin' Thru*, and on which he once again employs the word "crazy." With Gary on guitar, Greg on drums, Skip Olson on bass, and Michael Lewis on piano, it is the only track by what was the current touring edition of the band. Dino's "The Letter," sung with Kathi, features Gary on pedal steel guitar. Beginning as vaguely country before becoming a soulful number, Gary's "They Don't Know," again sung with Kathi, has an impressive instrumental break. "Flames," the only thing ever co-written by John and Dino—who both sing—includes John's brother Mario (future member of Huey Lewis & the News) on bass. The lead, drone, and feedback guitars instantly rekindle the sound of the "old" Quicksilver. The shortest track, "Witches' Moon," is an instrumental by Dino with more effective synthesizer from Michael, followed by the album's longest selection, Dino and Gary's "Bittersweet Love." Greg is given another brief moment in the sun, and the instrumental flourishes and dramatic finish are similar to something by the Who.

While the album was being mixed, Quicksilver played some dates in California, sometimes joined onstage by John, and though they lined up dates in Michigan and Texas, the days of widespread touring were over. At the end of 1975, John and the current lineup hit one of their old stomping grounds, Winterland, on December 28, the opening acts Sound Hole (with John's brother Mario on bass) and Little Feat. San Francisco historian Joel Selvin, author of the indispensable *Summer of Love*, attended the show for the Chronicle, which ran his review two days later with the headline "Quicksilver Slow to Warm Winterland": "The band made its first Bay Area appearance in more than two years Sunday night at Winterland, with less than two-thirds of the house filled...Cipollina joined his old colleagues...in a performance that rarely lifted itself above the mundane. Quicksilver never regained its prominence once guitarist Cipollina left to form his own band, Copperhead, although the band, in some form or another, continued to tour. Just to look at Gary Duncan was to know how long ago and far away it was when Quicksilver used to dedicate its version of Del Shannon's 'Runaway' to 'our friends in the Haight-Ashbury.' Duncan, who used to be the major force of the band's hippie/wild West image with his fringed jackets and the hunting knife on his belt, dressed like a dandy—long, billowing sleeves on his shirt, silk cravat at his neck, an earring dangling from one lobe. Quicksilver opened with 'Fresh Air' and followed that with a mangled version of 'Mona,' the sole selection of the evening from the band's golden days. Most of the material was drawn from the new album." (What Selvin neglected to mention was Greg's outstanding percussion on "Mona.")

In 2018, the Soundstage label issued a box set of Winterland concerts broadcast by KSAN-FM dating from 1967 and 1970 to the 1975 show, which made up two of the four discs. In addition to the numbers cited by Selvin, the band ran through such audience favorites as "Baby Baby," What About Me," "Freeway Flyer," "Subway," and "Who Do You Love." More than half the songs from *Solid Silver* were performed: "Gypsy Lights," "HeebieJeebies," "Cowboy on the Run," "Bittersweet Love," "They Don't Know," and "Worryin' Shoes," which was transformed into a tribal stomp that outclasses the studio version. The anonymous writer of the collection's booklet concluded, "This 1975 gig may have literally been the end of the line for the group, but it more often than not conveys a band that could still pull off performances as intense as ever. Despite their ups and downs over the years, these recordings

prove that Quicksilver's unique chemistry remained intact throughout. Valenti's unusual but undeniably expressive vocals are a major focal point here, but it's the unique understanding of rhythm and blues and rock and roll that the band as a whole brings together with an effective potency that is the beating heart of their legacy. This is Quicksilver Messenger Service as they always were and always will be."

In truth, the 1975 Winterland concert, a good example of Dino's showmanship, was not the end of the line for the band. One month into the New Year, January 31, they were recorded live at My Father's Place in Roslyn, New York, a performance that was kept under wraps until Purple Pyramid/Cleopatra Records included it in the *Live Across America 1967-1977* five-disc collection forty years later. Among the eight tracks are "Dr. Feelgood" (never recorded in the studio) and three from the reunion album: "Cowboy on the Run," "Bittersweet Love," and "They Don't Know." ("Baby Baby" is erroneously titled "The Truth.") As for still performing older songs, ace music historian Dave Thompson quoted Gary as saying the band's preferences were more important than what a crowd was clamoring for. "Why would you play a song you didn't like, just because the audience wanted to hear it? We didn't do things that way."

Quicksilver returned to My Father's Place later in 1976 (July 30 and 31) amid scattered dates around California, and closed the year by traveling to Germany to appear at a rock festival that included, among others, Procol Harum, Golden Earring, Rainbow, Scorpions, and John Cale. It was the first time they had crossed the Atlantic since 1972 as well as their final major performance anywhere.

After 1976, the band ceased to exist as an ongoing concern, reassembling in various configurations on rare occasions into the early Eighties. One of these events took place at the Quarter Note Lounge in New Orleans on July 26, 1977, and was released as a double-disc by Bear Records in 2009. (All fourteen tracks were winnowed down to a single CD for the Purple Pyramid box in 2016, the cardboard sleeve wrongly listing Greg, Skip, and Michael as still being in the band, though Thompson's notes are correct. Five other mistakes: "Dr. Feelgood" is called "Dr. Boogie," "I Just Can't Have You," is actually "Baby Baby," "Baby Baby" is "Subway" "Just a Country Boy" is "Rambling Gambler" and "Jump Back To Me" is "Gypsy Lights.") By 1977 Gary and Dino were joined by Rick Wetzel on bass, Chris Meyers on drums, and a musician identified as Captain Kirk on keyboards. Thompson described the show as a "treat…that blazes with a passion that utterly belies its late-in-the-day recording date, and even boasts a new song that never made it onto a new studio record, but which could have highlighted any of the band's past ones, 'I Want to Fly.' Where the show really hits pay dirt, though, is first, 'Mona,' revisiting the *Happy Trails* of the Bo Diddley catalog as though the band had never been away; and then, to close the evening, 'Who Do You Love,' spiraling, teasing, and as believable as ever. A reminder that, no matter what else had changed since the days of '67, some things…some statements…some declarations…stayed the same." One can't help but wonder if perhaps "I Want to Fly" would have been included in the Warner Bros. solo album Dino, regrettably, was never able to make. Two other non-studio songs included "Dr. Feelgood" and "Rambling Gambler."

The shows from 1976 and 1977 are, to date, the last recorded evidence of Quicksilver Messenger Service in its second decade, as well as the final recordings of Dino Valenti.

*

1980-2019

"When you say 'the band,' I consider the band the original four members."

Greg Elmore

DINO

In the late 1980s, Dino experienced a recurrence of some mental difficulties similar to those he had been treated for in the early 1960s, necessitating brain surgery for arteriovenous malformation. This resulted in some short-term memory loss and the need for medication to control convulsions. (A layman's diagnosis could conclude that Dino's mental condition may have been at least partly responsible for the unpredictable mood swings that made him hard to live with at times, yet also a joy to be around at others.) He continued to write songs and perform around Marin County, sometimes sitting in with fellow Bay Area artists, including a late '80s benefit at the Great American Music Hall, his final appearance. He passed away in his Santa Rosa home on November 16, 1994. "The night he died," his younger sister told the Rock & Roll Paradise website, "he called a lot of people…some of whom he hadn't talked to in quite a while. It's my understanding that it was all casual conversation, no revelations, or profundity, or theatrics, but more like he was saying hello one final time. I think, just as the Phoenix knows, he knew that his time was at hand, and being the 'Gypsy soul' that he was, must have felt that such an event was about to take place. I think, too, that he grew weary of his 'home' on this planet, and he felt he had done the best he could here, and was ready to try something else—see the next place, meet the next people, and move on. After all, Dino was a carnie."

He was also a very productive and often gifted songwriter, a folkie at heart, composer of no less than four rock standards—"Get Together," "Fresh Air," "What About Me," "Cowboy on the Run"—and at least that many—"Gone Again," "Hope," "Don't Cry My Lady Love," "The Truth"—that deserve to be remembered. His only solo album should have had a better fate and is a reminder of days when music mattered. Greg may feel Quicksilver without Dino was the real deal, but Dino is a substantial reason the band is more than a mere footnote in music history.

"All we did was ride motorcycles, get in fights," Gary said in reference to the time he and Dino spent wandering the country in 1969. "We just lived." Regarding their efforts to put together a band they were going to call the Outlaws, he said, "With Dino it was hard to get people to play with him. He didn't know how to play with other musicians at all." David echoed that belief. "He never should have been in a band. He was enormous by himself. The band really kind of diminished him."

From 2002 to 2004, Dino's son Joli and John's brother Mario played in a tribute band known as Quicksilver Gold.

*

DAVID

After the reunion of the original band in 1975, David resumed his full-time duties with Jefferson Starship, contributing to "Ozymandias" on *Spitfire* (1976), "Fire" on *Earth* (1978) and the radio hit "Jane" on *Freedom at Point Zero* (1979). By 1985, when the group renamed itself Starship and began incorporating the sterile sound of that decade's music, specifically the track "We Built This City," he split. "The only things real on that song were the vocals and the guitar," he said, "...it completely turned away from anything organic, and it wasn't really what I did. I was useless, so I left."

In 1986 he added backup vocals to three tracks on Gary's *Peace By Piece*, credited as being by Quicksilver and released only on vinyl by Capitol Records. Also helping out were former Quicksilver associates Kathi McDonald and Michael Lewis. Ten year later, David and Michael joined Gary for the first two volumes of a project called *Shapeshifter*, billed as Quicksilver 96. Another ten years on, the two appeared on *Snake Language* by Gary Duncan with Crawfish of Love, David on "narration" and Michael on keyboards. Also in 2006, David and Gary were recorded live at the Sweetwater in Mill Valley on June 7 for a show released on a double-disc by Bear Records in 2009 titled *Quicksilver Messenger Service Reunion* to commemorate the band's 40th anniversary. Joining on vocals was David's wife Linda Imperial. Among the eighteen well-recorded selections were the reliable standbys "Mona," "Pride of Man," "Gold and Silver," "Dino's Song," "Edward (The Mad Shirt Grinder)"—with Chris Smith on piano—"Gypsy Lights," and "Who Do You Love." Also exhumed were a pair of blues classics Quicksilver covered in their early days—"Killing Floor" and "Smokestack Lightning"—and David's "Harp Tree Lament" from his 1973 album with Paul Kantner and Grace Slick.

In 2005, David joined Paul Kantner's reunited Jefferson Starship, and on their 2007 *Jefferson's Tree of Liberty* album he revived Dino's "Cowboy on the Run."

Today, at the age of 87, he continues to perform under the banners of both Quicksilver and Jefferson Starship, whose 2020 album *Mother of the Sun* includes David's "Setting Sun," written with band member Cathy Richardson. In 2018, at the age of 80, he told *Rolling Stone*, "I feel confident we're doing the right thing. We want to keep the spirit of the band. It feels right. And I would like to do it as long as the world will let me. I'd rather die than retire."

*

JOHN

The Columbia album John recorded as part of the band Copperhead was released in 1973 to critical applause but anemic sales. Fortunately, it was reissued on CD in 2010, licensed by Sony to Floating World Records. Eight years later, a live performance by the band broadcast by KSAN-FM on January 23, 1972, was unearthed by the Air Cuts label.

Copperhead was far from John's only band following his time in Quicksilver, many of which were never recorded or made albums without John: Terry & the Pirates, Thunder & Lightning, Dinosaurs, Man,Problem Child, Zero, and Fish & Chips. Participating in some of these assemblages were Greg Elmore and such San Francisco vets as Spencer Dryden, Peter Albin, Barry Melton, and old buddy Nick

Gravenites. With the latter he toured Europe in 1980, well-documented on a trio of live albums (*Live in Athens at the Rodon*, *Monkey Medicine*, *Live at Rock Palast*) that feature such Quicksilver-associated tracks as "Pride of Man," "Who Do You Love," "Walkin' Blues," and Dino's "Get Together," credited to his real name, Chet Powers. The CD of their performance in Dortmund, Germany, also includes a DVD of the concert.

In 1991, two years after emphysema took him at age 45, *John Cipollina: Electric Guitar Slinger*, a video narrated by his sister Antonia, was released. On the cover he poses with a guitar, wearing a Mona Lisa smile, the Golden Gate Bridge in the background. The affectionate tribute includes interviews with numerous people whose lives he enriched, including Quicksilver band mates David, Nicky and Greg, and Dan Healy, Nick Gravenites, Bill Graham, Jerry Garcia, Paul Kantner, and others. There are anecdotes about John's dark sense of humor, his love of fans, and how he rigged Quicksilver's practice house in Corte Madera to explode when the fire department burned it down for practice by putting gunpowder in the walls.

No longer available except on the secondary market is Culture Factory's three-DVD *Recoil: John Cipollina "In Music and In Memory."* In addition to *Electric Guitar Slinger* are nearly five more hours of interviews and nineteen concert performances by John with Quicksilver, Copperhead, Link Wray, Thunder & Lightning, Dinosaurs, and Terry & the Pirates. Ten albums by the latter have been released, all but one (*The Doubtful Handshake*, recorded in 1980 and issued on CD in 2010 by MIG Music) only on the secondary market. Greg is on board for one (*West Coast Legends-Vol. 5*, recorded live in 1982 and released on CD in 2011), Nicky on another (*Comanche Boots*, issued on CD in 2008). He also appeared on a live album in 1975, *Maximum Darkness*, with the Welsh band Man, which a critic once compared to the Grateful Dead and Quicksilver. Selections included renditions of the first two tracks Quicksilver ever recorded: "Codine" and "Babe, I'm Gonna Leave You." (Listed in the Discography are several obscure releases either readily unavailable or quite expensive.)

Today John is remembered for a number of innovations, especially his amplifier rig, a combination transistor/tube stereo tower, topped with horns and flashing lights. He pioneered the now-common concept of twin lead guitars. "We got into double leads right from the start, partly at my insistence," he said. "I've always liked double leads, and just because no one was doing double leads at the time, it didn't stop us." John and Gary employed different styles and tones, which served to intensify the effect. Even so, John—who was on all but two of the band's seven Capitol albums—was to say on more than one occasion, "I don't think the group ever reached its potential."

In 2003, Rolling Stone ranked John as the #32 greatest guitarist of all-time, referring to Quicksilver Messenger Service as "the best acid rock dance band of the Sixties." (John was nowhere to be found on an updated list of the best guitarists the magazine published eight years later.)

*

GARY

More than any of the band members, Gary did the most to keep Quicksilver name alive, sharing music and photographs from his personal archives with independent labels. After the reunion album,

Gary, Dino, and Greg (with Michael Lewis on keyboards and Skip Olson on bass) played sporadic dates until 1983, sometimes with Nick Gravenites and billed as Nicksilver. Frustrated by the lack of forward momentum and the music industry in general, Gary decided to call it a day, as he had in 1969, and entered the labor market as a dock worker. Former Hot Tuna and Stoneground drummer Sammy Piazza, in an interview with Jefferson Airplane authority Craig Fenton, filled in some of the blanks in Quicksilver's history after debunking rumors that he had been a part of the sessions for 1969's *Shady Grove*: "…I first met the guys from Quicksilver at the time of the reunion record *Solid Silver*. A friend of mine, Skip Olson, was playing bass. He is no longer living. That is really the way I met Gary Duncan. When I was in Hot Tuna we didn't hang out with Quicksilver. Most of the hanging was with the Grateful Dead and the New Riders of the Purple Sage. There were different musical camps…When I got out of Stoneground, Gary called me up and said 'If you need some bread my wife's aunt owns a freight service. It's hard work, but I can get you into the union. It will be you, and me, and three other guys.' At that point he wasn't doing anything. I got hurt there. I slipped a disc and needed an operation."

Gary, at Sammy's urging, returned to the music arena in 1984 as Gary Duncan's Quicksilver, which was possibly when he and Greg had their dispute over ownership of the name. "I told Gary that we should get some money for a musical project and I had a good engineer," said Sammy. "His name was Bob Ohlsson, who did the Marvin Gaye *What's Going On* album. He was great. He worked for Motown and knew what he was doing." The trio leased the necessary recording equipment, put a studio together, and the end result was the album *Peace By Piece*, released by Capitol in 1986. Gary had evidently put aside his ill will toward the company, which resurrected its famous "rainbow" label for the album. Assisted by former original member David, as well as latter day Quicksilver keyboard artist Michael Lewis, singer Kathi McDonald, and Sammy on percussion, Gary was back in his element. "I produced the entire thing," said Sammy, though the production credits included Gary and Bob. "I arranged the entire thing, listened to everything that went on there, and Gary wrote the majority of the songs. We couldn't do it without each other. I mean, Gary, Bob, and I…Most of the stuff was live. We spliced a couple of things. Now, my forte is production. I went to Fantasy Studios to make some safety copies of the album." *Peace By Piece* suffered the same lack of promotion as most of Quicksilver's releases. (This author found it by accident that year in a Los Angeles record store. Coincidentally, it was filed along with the 1968 *Revolution* soundtrack.) The surprisingly wide-ranging and even melodic collection of eight songs starts off with "Good Thang," which could possibly be a put-down of Dino, depending on how the listener wants to interpret it. "Pool Hall Chili" smacks of Bo Diddley, and the title song bows to the 1980s with some rapping. Fortunately, the use of the synthesizer, increasingly mandatory on albums of the era, is not intrusive. Unfortunately, it has never been issued on CD.

In addition to 1996's first two (of four) volumes of the *Shapeshifter* series, recorded with the help of David, Michael Lewis, David's wife Linda Imperial, and many others (including War's Lee Oskar), Gary released several albums either as Quicksilver or under his own name until 2010. (See Discography) While some are, like John's post-Quicksilver output, difficult to track down or afford, his 1996 efforts, the live 2006 reunion with David, and a few others are available. These include 2006's *Snake Language* (with Crawfish of Love, including a remake of "Calvary"), 2007's *Six String Voodoo*, and his final album, 2010's *The Hermit*. All are wildly eclectic, reflecting Gary's fondness for jazz and blues.

When asked in later years about his yearlong defection from Quicksilver in 1969, he noted a lack of ambition on the part of his fellow musicians, particularly during recording sessions. "After we got our first record," he added, "everybody had enough money to get their own place and we stopped playing together."

It was not the last time he would turn his back on the music business, again "retiring" from performing and recording in 2001, going so far as ripping up his home studio. "I tore the studio apart by myself, no help from any of my friends. In fact, not even a word. They all came and got the stuff they had stored and left the stuff they didn't want so I could haul it away, and they just never spoke to me again."

In 2004 Gary resumed his music career and remained active until he had a seizure and several cardiac arrests in June of 2019. He lapsed into a coma for ten days, dying on June 29 in Woodland, California, without regaining consciousness. "I don't think he ever stopped playing," said David. "He was a real unusual guy who was full of tales. He was a sailor. He was a cowboy. He had a lot of spirituality." A mark of his devotion to the band, as well as his perseverance, is the fact that he was one of the few people who sincerely befriended and could hold his own against the overwhelming powerhouse Dino Valenti.

Gary's passing, unlike Jerry Garcia's nearly 25 years before, was not a major news event. There were no national headlines or respectful tributes, nor did he appear on the cover of any music publication. His snarling, imaginative guitar work on such outstanding tracks as "Calvary," "Fresh Air," "The Truth," and so many others deserves to be remembered. His compositions "I Found Love" and "Doin' Time in the U.S.A" should have been singles as recognizable today as "Fresh Air" and "What About Me?" Fortunately, much of what Gary—and Quicksilver—accomplished is still available and worthy of discovery by any music enthusiast who has never heard the band. For those of us who were there, Quicksilver Messenger Service stands as an iconic representation of the days when music truly mattered—an era long over, yet never to be forgotten. Let your freak flag fly!

*

DISCOGRAPHY

The majority of the recordings listed here are reasonably easy to find, either new or on the secondary market. With the exception of the elusive Greg Elmore album, this author owns and has heard them all. The quality of the sound and the music itself are, of course, up to the individual listener.

1966

Live In San Jose 1966 (09/2-3/66) I.E.S. Hall, San Jose, CA (Purple Pyramid/Cleopatra Records, 2015): All Night Worker, Walkin' Blues, I Hear You Knockin', If You Live (Your Time Will Come), Smokestack Lightning, Who Do You Love, Back Door Man, Acapulco Gold & Silver, Cod'ine, The Fool

Live At the Avalon Ballroom (09-09-66) San Francisco, CA (Bear Records, 2008): Radio Commercial, Stand By Me, Babe I'm Gonna Leave You, Pride of Man, Smokestack Lightning, Codeine, Gold and Silver, Hoochie Coochie Man

Live At the Avalon Ballroom (10-28-66) San Francisco, CA (Bear Records, 2008): Band Intro, Mona, If You Live Your Time Will Come, Smokestack Lightning, Dandelion, Codeine, Runaway, Pride of Man

Fillmore Auditorium (11-05-66) San Francisco, CA (Purple Pyramid/Cleopatra Records, 2014): Dino's Song, Hair Like Sunshine (Long Distance Call), I Hear You Knockin', Babe, I'm Gonna Leave You, Smokestack Lightnin', If You Live (Your Time Will Come), All Night Worker, Got My Mojo Workin', You Don't Love Me, Susie Q,

Hoochie Coochie Man, Acapulco Gold and Silver, Stand By Me, Pride of Man

1967

Live At the Fillmore Auditorium (02-04-67) San Francisco (Bear Records, 2008): You Don't Love Me, I Hear You Knocking, Gold and Silver, All Night Worker, Codeine, Got My Mojo Working, Mona, A Fool For You, I Can't Believe It, Look Around (Excerpt), Dino's Song, Walkin' Blues, Babe I'm Gonna Leave You, Hoochie Coochie Man, Stand By Me, Drivin' Wheel (It's Been Too Long), Duncan and Brady, Pride of Man, Who Do You Love

Fillmore Auditorium (02-05-67) San Francisco (Purple Pyramid/Cleopatra Records, 2015)-2 Discs: Suzy Q, I Hear You Knockin' Dandelion, Acapulco Gold & Silver, You Don't Love Me, Cod'ine, Instrumental, Smokestack Lightnin', Dino's Song, Walkin' Blues, Drivin' Wheel (It's Been Too Long), Babe I'm Gonna Leave You, Hey Mama, Hoochie Coochie Man, All Night Worker, Stand By Me, Pride of Man

Live At the Summer of Love (Fourteen tracks from 02-04-67 at the Fillmore Auditorium, six undated tracks recorded at the Carousel Ballroom, two tracks Fillmore tracks dated 02-06-67 actually from either the 4th or 5th as the Auditorium was closed on the 6th)-2 Discs: Mona, Walkin' Blues, Codeine, Babe I'm Gonna Leave You, Gold and Silver, Dino's Song, Back Door Man, I Hear You Knocking, Pride of Man, Light Your Windows, Hoochie Coochie Man, Year of the Outrage, Duncan and Brady, The Fool, I

Can't Believe It, Who Do You Love, All Night Worker, Drivin' Wheel (It's Been Too Long), Stand By Me, A Fool For You, You Don't Love Me, Hey Mama

Live At the Fillmore Auditorium (02-06-67) San Francisco (Bear Records, 2008) Recorded on either the 4th or 5th, not the 6th: You Don't Love Me, All Night Worker, Gold and Silver, Hey Mama, Walkin' Blues, Year of the Outrage, I Hear You Knocking, A Fool For You, I Can't Believe It

New Year's Eve 1967: Winterland Auditorium, San Francisco (Purple Pyramid/Cleopatra, 2015): Instrumental, Pride of Man, Who Do You Love, If You Live (Your Time Will Come), It's Been Too Long, Smokestack Lightning, Babe I'm Gonna Leave You, Gold and Silver, Dino's Song, Back Door Man, Mona/Maiden of the Cancer Moon

1968

Live At the Carousel Ballroom (02-04-68) San Francisco (Bear Records, 2008)-2 Discs: Quicksilver was in Oregon on 02-04-68, not San Francisco. This performance is likely from January 17: Back Door Man, Light Your Windows, Who Do You Love, Babe I'm Gonna Leave You, Walkin' Blues, The Fool

Quicksilver Messenger Service (Capitol Records, May 1968) (Capitol, 1988 CD): Pride of Man, Light Your Windows, Dino's Song, Gold and Silver, Too Long, The Fool

Live At the Fillmore (06-07-68) New York (Purple Pyramid/Cleopatra Records/Freakbeat Records, 2013)-2 Discs (Licensed from the archives of Gary Duncan): Quicksilver's first concert at the Fillmore East: Pride of Man, If You Live (Your Time Will Come), Dino's Song, Smokestack Lightnin', Codine, Light Your Windows, Mona, Calvary, Back Door Man, Acapulco Gold & Silver, Who Do You Love, The Fool

Winterland, November 1968 (11-07-68) San Francisco (Sonic Boom, 2014) Recorded at the Fillmore West, not Winterland: Mona, Smokestack Lightning, Who Do You Love?, Susie Q, I Get In Trouble, Stand By Me

1969

Happy Trails (Capitol Records, March 1969) (Capitol CD, 1988): Who Do You Love—Part 1, When You Love, Where You Love, How You Love, Which Do You Love, Who Do You Love—Part 2, Mona, Maiden of the Cancer Moon, Calvary, Happy Trails

More Happy Trails (12-31-69) Winterland, San Francisco (Purple Pyramid/Cleopatra Records, 2016): Subway, I Believe, Words Can't Say, Mojo, Mona, City of Stone, Edward the Mad Shirt Grinder

Castles in the Sand (Late 1969/Early 1970 rehearsals, demos) Charly/Artistry Music Limited, 2009): Senor Blues, Subway, I Know You Rider #1, I Know You Rider #2, Walk In Jerusalem, Castles in the Sand, May You Never Be Alone, Warm Red Wine, Look Over Yonder Wall/State Farm, Wake Up, Dead Man (Part 1), Wake, Dead Man (Part 2), The Fool

Shady Grove (Capitol Records, December 1969) (One Way Records/Cema CD, 1990): Shady Grove, Flute Song, 3 or 4 Feet From Home, Too Far, Holy Moly, Joseph's Coat, Flashing Lonesome, Words Can't Say, Edward (The Mad Shirt Grinder)

1970

Live At the Old Mill Tavern (03-29-70) Mill Valley, CA (Purple Pyramid/Cleopatra Records, 2013): Subway, The Truth, Mona, Baby Baby, Rain, Mojo, Blues Jam #1, Blues Jam #2

Stony Brook College (04-05-70) New York (Purple Pyramid/ Cleopatra Records, 2015) Issued under exclusive license from Richie Blackmore-2 Discs: Baby Baby, Subway, Too Far, Warm Red Wine, The Truth, Mona, Long Haired Lady, Mojo, Pride of Man, Edward the Mad Shirt Grinder, Who Do You Love

Hawaii 1970 (06-13-70) Honolulu Convention Center (Gonzo Multimedia, 2014) With limited edition bonus disc of 06-04-70 rehearsal at the Opaelua Lodge in Haleiwa, Hawaii. Special thanks to Gary Duncan for supplying the sleeve photographs: Fresh Air (Excerpt), Warm Red Wine, Subway, Pride of Man, Baby Baby, The Hat, Edward…, The Truth, Freeway Flyer, Mojo. **Rehearsal:** Cobra, Guitar Jam, Won't Kill Me, Cobra (Acoustic), Good Old Rock and Roll, Drums, Just For Love

Just For Love (Capitol Records, July 1970) (BGO Records/EMI CD, 1992): Wolf Run (Part 1), Just For Love (Part 1), Cobra, The Hat, Freeway Flyer, Gone Again, Fresh Air, Just For Love (Part 2), Wolf Run (Part 2)

At the Kabuki Theatre (12-31-70) San Francisco (Charly/Artistry Music Limited, 2007) With four bonus tracks from 1969 studio rehearsal (2 Discs): Fresh Air, New Year's Jam, Baby Baby, Too Far, Truth, You're Gonna Need Somebody On Your Bond **(misspelled "Band" by Charly)**, Doctor Feelgood, Cobra, Song For Frisco, Mona, Subway, What About Me, Call On Me, Pride of Man, Local Color, Not Fade Away, Mojo, Freeway Flyer

1971

What About Me (Capitol Records, December 1970) (BGO Records/EMI CD, 1990): What About Me, Local Color, Baby Baby, Won't Kill Me, Long Haired Lady, Subway, Spindrifter, Good Old Rock and Roll, All In My Mind, Call On Me

Independence Day 1971 (07-03-71, not July 4) Fillmore West (Carlotta's CDs, Australia, Undated): Introduction, Fresh Air, Baby Baby, Dr. Feelgood, Too Much To Say **(Words Can't Say)**, Mona, Subway, Ain't That A Shame, Doin' Time in the USA, Mojo, Come On Along, The Truth, Road Runner, The Hat, Who Do You Love, What About Me, Call On Me, Motorcycle Blues

Quicksilver (Capitol Records, November 1971) (One Way Records/Cema CD, 1993): Hope, I Found Love, Song For Frisco, Play My Guitar, Rebel, Fire Brothers, Out of My Mind, Don't Cry My Lady Love, The Truth

1972

Comin' Thru (Capitol Records, April 1972) (BGO Records/EMI CD, 1991): Doin' Time In the U.S.A., Chicken, Changes, California State Correctional Facility Blues, Forty Days, Mojo, Don't Lose It

Fillmore: The Last Days (Fillmore Corporation/Columbia Records, July 1972) QMS on two tracks: Fresh Air, Mojo

1973

Live At the Winterland Ballroom (12-01-73) San Francisco (Purple Pyramid/Cleopatra Records, 2013): Losing Hand, Play My Guitar, Mojo, What About Me, The Hat, Who Do You Love?, Jam 1, Jam 2

1975

Solid Silver (Capitol Records, October 1975) (Edsel Records/ EMI CD, 2000): Gypsy Lights, HeebieJeebies, Cowboy On the Run, I Heard You Singing, Worryin' Shoes, The Letter, They Don't Know, Flames, Witches' Moon, Bittersweet Love

1977

Live At the Quarter Lounge (07-26-77) New Orleans, LA (Bear Records, 2009)-2 Discs (Gary Duncan and Dino Valenti only original members): Fresh Air, Dr. Feelgood, Baby Baby, Mona, Play My Guitar, Gypsy Lights, Cowboy On the Run, Bittersweet Love, What About Me?, Freeway Flyer, I Wanna Fly, Subway, Rambling Gambler, Who Do You Love?

1986

Peace By Piece (Capitol) Gary Duncan and David Freiberg only original members: Good Thang, 24 Hour Déjà vu, Midnight Sun, Swamp Girl, Wild in the City, Pool Hall Chili, Pistolero, Peace By Piece

1996

Shape Shifter Vol. 1 & Vol. 2 (Pymander Records)- 2 Discs: Credited to Quicksilver 96, Gary Duncan and David Freiberg only original members: Rebel, Big Bright Street, The Dog Song, Bubba Jeans, Life is So Funky, Angeline, Carnival Time in Nicaragua, I Don't Want To Hear It Anymore, Don't Go To Strangers, Richmond Welfare Strut, Nobody But You, We'll Be Together, Tattoo, Rex Dark, King-O-China, Snowman/Nica's Dream, The Fatman, Steve McQueen, Close Enuf For Jazz, Please Don't Touch the Tip,

Gangster Purple, Vera Cruz, What Did You Do To Yo Do?, Jackie Boy, Blue Weasel On Ice, Hoochie Coochie Man, Sugar Pie, Holiday

2006

Reunion (06-07-06) The Sweetwater, Mill Valley, CA (Bear Records, 2009)-2 Discs (Gary Duncan and David Freiberg only original members): Vera Cruz, Edward, Mona, Pride of Man, Steve McQueen, Gold

& Silver, I Don't Want To Live In Fear, Bubba Jeans, Dino's Song, Edward the Mad Shirt Grinder, Vera Cruz, Gypsy Lights, Holiday, Who Do You Love, Harp Tree Lament, Killing Floors, Close Enough For Jazz, Smokestack Lightning

2007

Six String Voodoo (Global Recording Artists) Gary Duncan only original member: Katmandu, Round Midnight, Pharoah's Dance, Baghdad Boogie, Don't Be Lonely, Ant's Romance, Sketches of Blavatsky

2010

The Hermit (Global Recording Artists) Gary Duncan only original member: Nica's Dream, Samba Triste/Green Dolphin Street, Vera Cruz Inst., Cancion Para Dios, Boo-Hooin' A Night In Tunisia, Selling Miss Murphy, El Dorado Inst.

COMPILATIONS

Quicksilver Anthology (Capitol, 1973) / (BGO Records, 1995)-2 Discs: Pride of Man, Dino's Song, The Fool, Bears, Mona, Edward the Mad Shirt Grinder, Three or Four Feet From Home, Fresh Air, Just For Love, Spindrifter, Local Color, What About Me, Don't Cry My Lady Love, Hope, Fire Brothers, I Found Love

The Best of Quicksilver Messenger Service (Capitol, 1990): Who Do You Love, What About Me, Shady Grove, Just For Love, Fresh Air, Pride of Man, Dino' Song, Joseph's Coat, Long Haired Lady, California State Correctional Facility Blues, Stand By Me

The Best of Quicksilver Messenger Service: Sons of Mercury (Capitol/Rhino Records, 1991)-2 Discs: Babe I'm Gonna Leave You, Codine, I Hear You Knockin' (It's Too Late), Pride of Man, Light Your Windows, Dino's Song, The Fool, Gold And Silver, Bears, Who Do You Love, Mona, Maiden of the Cancer Moon, Calvary, Happy Trails, Shady Grove, Flute Song, Joseph's Coat, Edward the Mad Shirt Grinder, Fresh Air, Cobra, Subway, What About Me, Local Color, Hope, Fire Brothers, Don't Cry My Lady Love, I Found Love, Doin' Time In the U.S.A., Gypsy Lights, Cowboy On the Run

Unreleased Quicksilver Messenger Service: Lost Gold and Silver (EMI-Capitol Music/Collectors' Choice, 1999)-2 Discs: Back Door Man, Codine, Gold & Silver, Smokestack Lightning, Light Your Windows, Dino's Song, The Fool, Who Do You Love, Mona/ Maiden of the Cancer Moon, I Don't Want To Spoil Your Party (Dino's Song), Acapulco Gold and Silver (Gold and Silver), I Hear You Knockin', Back Door Man, Your Time Will Come, Who Do

You Love (Part 1), Walkin' Blues, Calvary, Codine, Babe I'm Gonna Leave You, Stand By Me, The Bears

Quicksilver Messenger Service: Classic Masters (Capitol, 2002): Pride of Man, Light Your Windows, Who Do You Love (Part 1), Stand By Me, Dino's Song, Shady Grove, Joseph's Coat, Flute Song, Fresh Air, What About Me, Just For Love, Hope **(Song selection nearly identical to 1990 and 2006 compilations)**

The Best of Quicksilver Messenger Service (Capitol, 2006): Reissue of the 1990 collection with a different cover and no liner notes

Quicksilver Messenger Service Anthology Box 1966-1970 (Cleopatra Records, 2011)-3 CDs/1 DVD: 1967-69 Studio Outtakes, Live (Fillmore Auditorium: 05-11-66 & 02-04-67), Live 1968-1970 (Fillmore East, Winterland, Old Mill Tavern), DVD: Monterey International Pop Festival, *Revolution* tracks, Sonoma State College, Fillmore West, Winterland Ballroom)

Quicksilver Messenger Service: The CD Vinyl Replica Collection (Capitol/Culture Factory, 2015)-7 Discs: All the original Capitol albums except *Solid Silver*

Quicksilver Messenger Service: Live Across America 1967-1977 (Cleopatra Records, 2016)-5 Discs: Fillmore Auditorium 1967, Red Vest Inn 1970, My Father's Place 1976, Quarter Note 1977, Opaelua Lodge Rehearsal 1970

Quicksilver Messenger Service: Winterland 1967-1975 (Soundstage, 2018)-4 Discs: December 1967, April 1970, December 1975

Quicksilver: Sweet California Sunshine-Vol. 1 (Japan, 2023)-6 Discs: Live At the Matrix (08/66), Fillmore West (09-04-66), Matrix (03-19-67), Demos and Rehearsals 1967 and 1969

Quicksilver: Sweet California Sunshine-Vol. 2 (Japan, 2023)-6 Discs: Live At Fillmore Auditorium (02/67)

Quicksilver: Sweet California Sunshine-Vol. 3 (Japan, 2023)-6 Discs: Live On KSAN-FM (04-01-68) Winterland (12-31-67), Matrix (10-21-70), "The Fool" Outtakes and Rehearsals (12/9-11/67)

Quicksilver Messenger Service: Rare Tracks-Limited Edition (Cleopatra Records, 2011 & 2023): Dino's Song, Acapulco Gold & Silver #1, Light Your Windows, Pride of Man, I Hear You Knockin', Stand By Me #1, Stand By Me #2, The Fool, Acapulco Gold & Silver #2, Calvary, Who Do You Love (Exclusive Mix)

RELATED SELECTIONS

DINO VALENTI

Dino Valente (Epic, August 1968) (Koch/Sony, 1998)

Get Together: The Lost Recordings Pre-1970 (It's About Music, 2011)

Get Together Bonus Disc (It's About Music, 2011)

NICK GRAVENITES

My Labors (Columbia, 1969) (Retroworld/Sony, 2010) "Anonymous Friends" on three tracks allegedly include members of Quicksilver Messenger Service

JOHN CIPOLLINA

Mickey Hart: Rolling Thunder (Warner Bros., 1972) (Grateful Dead Records, 1990)

Copperhead Live At Pacific High Studios, San Francisco, 1972 (Aircuts, 2018)

Copperhead (Columbia, 1973) (Floating World Records/Sony, 2010)

Man: Maximum Darkness (Esoteric Recordings, 2008)

Terry & the Pirates: The Doubtful Handshake 1980 (MIG Music, 2010)

Terry & the Pirates: West Coast Legends-Vol. 5, 1982 (MIG Music, 2011)

Terry & the Pirates: Return to Silverado-Vol 1 (Acadia Records, 2007)

Terry & the Pirates: Too Close for Comfort (Acadia Records, 2008)

Terry & the Pirates: Comanche Boots (Acadia Records, 2008)

Live In Athens at the Rodon w/Nick Gravenites 1980 (It's About Music, 2011)

Monkey Medicine w/Nick Gravenites 1980 (It's About Music, 2011)

Live At Rockpalast 1980 w/Nick Gravenites (MIG Music, 2018)-2 CDs/1 DVD

(Other releases featuring John that are either out-of-print or pricey)

Copperhead: Born, Live & Die Like A Hero

John Cipollina: Wander Far & Wide-Vol. 1

John Cipollina: Wander Far & Wide-Vol. 2

John Cipollina: Legacy Live

Problem Child: It's Not My Fault

Dinosaurs (1988)

Zero: Here Goes Nothin' (Relix Records, 1987)

Zero: Nothin' Goes Here (Mobile Fidelity, 1990)

Zero: Go Hear Nothin' (Whirled Records, 1991)

Terry & The Pirates: Wind Dancer (Rag Baby/Line Records, 1981)

Terry & the Pirates: Rising of the Moon (Rag Baby/Line Records, 1982)

Terry & the Pirates: Acoustic Rangers (Sawdust Records, 1987)

Terry & the Pirates: Silverado Trail (Big Beat Records, 1990)

Terry & the Pirates: Return to Silverado—Vol. 2 (Acadia Records, 2011)

Raven: John Cipollina's Raven (Line Records, 1980)

DAVID FREIBERG

David Crosby: If I Could Only Remember My Name (Atlantic, 1971) (Atlantic/Rhino, 2021)-2 Discs

Mickey Hart: Rolling Thunder (Warner Bros., 1972) (Grateful Dead Records, 1990)

Jefferson Airplane: Thirty Seconds Over Winterland 1972 (Grunt/RCA, 1973) (Icon Classic/Sony, 2009)

Jefferson Airplane: Last Flight 1972 (Charly/Artistry Music Limited, 2007)

Paul Kantner, Grace Slick, David Freiberg: Baron Von Tollbooth & The Chrome Nun (Grunt/RCA, 1973) (RCA/BMG, 1997) Includes David's "Harp Tree Lament" (co-written by Robert Hunter) and the title song (co-written by Grace Slick)

Jefferson Starship: Dragonfly (Grunt/RCA, 1974) (Sony/BMG, 2007) Includes David's "Come To Life" (co-written by Robert Hunter and Stephen Schuster)

Jefferson Starship: Red Octopus (RCA, 1975) (Grunt/Rhino, 2023)-Quadio Disc. Includes David's "Tumblin'" (co-written by Marty Balin and Robert Hunter)

Jefferson Starship: Live In Central Park NYC May 12, 1975 (RCA/Sony/Real Gone Music, 2013) Includes David's "Come To Life" (co-written by Robert Hunter)

Jefferson Starship: Spitfire (Grunt/RCA, 1976) (BMG/RCA/Grunt, 2004) Includes David's "Ozymandias" (co-written by Paul Kantner, Craig Chaquico, John Barbata, Pete Sears and Grace Slick)

Jefferson Starship: Earth (Grunt/RCA, 1978) (BMG/RCA, 1997) Includes David's "Fire" (co-written by Buchwald/Robbins/Sears)

Jefferson Starship: Jefferson's Tree of Liberty (Lab Records/Great American Music Company, 2015) Includes Dino Valenti's "Cowboy On the Run."

Jefferson Starship: Mother of the Sun (Secret Knock, 2020) Includes David's "Setting Sun" (co-written by Cathy Richardson)

GARY DUNCAN

Crawfish of Love: Snake Language (Global Recording Artists, 2006) With David Freiberg

NOTE: There are other albums released as either Gary Duncan's Quicksilver or under Gary's name (Strange Trim, Shapeshifter 3 & 4, Live At Fieldstone, Live '07, Three In the Side) that are difficult to find or afford

GREG ELMORE

Terry & the Pirates: West Coast Legends-Vol. 5, 1982 (MIG, 2011)

Little Joe (A September 1985 issue of Goldmine mentions this album, about which no further information could be found)

NICKY HOPKINS

The Revolutionary Piano of Nicky Hopkins (Columbia, 1966)

Nicky Hopkins Caravan: Hammond On the Rocks (Volksplatte, 1969)

Nicky Hopkins: Jamming With Edward (Rolling Stones Records, 1972)

The Tin Man Was A Dreamer (Columbia, 1973) (Virgin Records, 1997)

No More Changes (Mercury, 1975)

Jerry Garcia Band: Let It Rock 1975 (Rhino, 2009) Includes Nicky's "Pig's Boogie" and "Edward, the Mad Shirt Grinder"

*

BIBLIOGRAPHY

BOOKS

Churton, Tobias. *The Spiritual Meaning of the Sixties*. Rochester, VE: Inner Traditions, 2018.

Crosby, David and Gottleib, Carl. *Long Time Gone: The Autobiography of David Crosby*. New York: Doubleday, 1988.

Dawson, Julian. *and on piano...Nicky Hopkins: The Extraordinary Life of Rock's Greatest Session Man*. San Francisco, CA: Backstage Press, 2011.

Duncan, Shelley L. *My Husband the Rock Star: Ten Years with Quicksilver Messenger Service*. Merced, CA: Flower Child Books, 2002.

Fenton, Craig. *Take Me to a Circus Tent: The Jefferson Airplane Flight Manual*. West Conshohocken, PA: Infinity Publishing Company, 2007.

Gasser, Nolan. *Why You Like It: The Science & Culture of Musical Taste*. New York: Flatiron Books, 2019.

Gilmore, Mikal. *Stories Done: Writings on the Sixties and Its Discontents*. New York: Free Press/Simon & Schuster, 2008.

Gleason, Ralph J. *The Jefferson Airplane and the San Francisco Sound*. New York: Bantam Books, 1969.

Gleason, Ralph J. *Music in the Air: The Selected Writings of Ralph J. Gleason*. New Haven, CT/London: Yale University Press, 2016.

Goldstein, Richard. *Goldstein's Greatest Hits*. NY: Tower Publications, Inc., 1970.

Hjort, Christopher. *So You Want to Be a Rock 'n' Roll Star: The Byrds Day-By-Day 1965-1973*. London: Outline Press/Jawbone Books, 2008.

Jack, Richard Morton. *Psychedelia: 101 Iconic Underground Rock Albums*. NY: Sterling Publishers, 2017.

Jackson, Blair. *The Music Never Stopped*. New York: Deliah Communications, Ltd., 1983.

Jackson, Blair. *Garcia: An American Life*. New York: Viking/Penguin Group, 1999.

Lesh, Phil. *Searching for the Sound: My Life with the Grateful Dead*. New York: Little, Brown & Co., 2005.

Perry, Charles. *The Haight-Ashbury: A History*. New York: Wenner Books, 2005.

Pollock, Bruce. *When the Music Mattered: Rock in the 1960s*. New York: Holt, Rinehart & Winston, 1984.

McNally, Dennis. *A Long Strange Trip: The Inside History of the Grateful Dead*. New York: Broadway Books/Random House, 2002.

Scully, Rock and Dalton, David. *Living with the Dead*. New York: Little, Brown & Co., 1996.

Selvin, Joel. *Summer of Love*. New York: Plume, 1995.

Tamarkin, Jeff. *Got A Revolution! The Turbulent Flight of Jefferson Airplane*. New York: Atria Books, 2003.

Troy, Sandy. *Captain Trips: A Biography of Jerry Garcia*. New York: Thunder's Mouth Press, 1994.

Troy, Sandy. *One More Saturday Night*. New York: St. Martin's Press, 1991.

Warren, Holly-George. *Janis: Her Life and Music*. New York: Simon & Schuster, 2019.

Willis, Ellen. *Out of the Vinyl Deeps*. Minneapolis, MN: University of Minnesota Press, 2011.

Wolkin, Jan Mark & Keenom, Bill. *Michael Bloomfield: If You Love These Blues*. San Francisco, CA: Miller Freeman Books, 2000.

Editors of Rolling Stone. *Rock Almanac: The Chronicles of Rock & Roll*. New York: Collier Books/Macmillan Publishing Company, 1983.

*

Periodicals:

Circus

Crawdaddy

Fusion

Goldmine

Hit Parader

Relix

Rock

Rolling Stone

Stereo Review

Uncut

Zoo World

ABOUT THE AUTHOR

David R. Greenland has been writing professionally for more than 50 years. His work has appeared in newspapers and magazines, including Classic Images, the oldest film publication in the country, to which he contributes two monthly columns. He has taught creative writing at a local college and is the author of four books published by BearManor Media (*Bonanza: A Viewer's Guide to the TV Legend*, *Rawhide: A History of Television's Longest Cattle Drive*, *The Gunsmoke Chronicles: A New History of Television's Greatest Western*, *Michael Landon: The Career and Artistry of a Television Genius*). He is also the co-author of *Inside the Fire: My Strange Days With the Doors* by B. Douglas Cameron. His lifelong addiction to music has resulted in a collection of titles on vinyl and CD numbering in the thousands, as well as several hundred books of music history. A one-time resident of Los Angeles, he now lives in his home state of Illinois.

www.ingramcontent.com/pod-product-compliance
Ingram Content Group UK Ltd.
Pitfield, Milton Keynes, MK11 3LW, UK
UKHW021910190726
13853UKWH00002B/606